Being green is more than just buying eco. It is an unshakable commitment to a sustainable lifestyle.

A catalogue record of this book is available from the National Library of Australia.

Messenger, Lisa. 365 Days of Sustainability
ISBN 978-0-6485872-7-9
First published in 2020 by The Messenger Group Pty Ltd
Project Management: @em.lystudio
Editing: Lucy Pearson and Victoria Kingsbury
Proofreading: Claire Hey
Creative Direction and Design: @em.lystudio
Distribution Enquiries: lisam@collectivehub.com

This is proudly a Lisa Messenger product, lisamessenger.com

365 days of sustainability

TIPS & TECHNIQUES FOR CONSCIOUS LIVING

LISA MESSENGER

FOUNDER AND EDITOR-IN-CHIEF OF *COLLECTIVE HUB*

introduction

The notion of living a conscious, sustainable and ethical life has long been something I've been passionate about. I'm constantly trying to do better, be better and, in turn, I also hope to inspire others to assess their own lifestyle habits. But I don't always get it right, far from it. In this day and age we are bombarded on a daily – sometimes hourly – basis with things and ways in which we could be doing better; better ways to save the planet, better ways to eat, better ways to give back. With this constant tirade of often conflicting messages, it's easy to feel overwhelmed, powerless and incapable of making any real impact. More often than not, it's easier to simply bury our heads in the sand and disregard or overlook the fact that together, collectively, we really can bring about change for the better.
I want to address those feelings of overwhelm and helplessness, and so, on the back of the success of our recent new formats of 'how to' inspirational and educational books, my team and I thought we'd put together another little book filled with 365 tips of some small ways you can make a difference.

So, this book provides a road map of thought-starters, ideas, places and spaces you could explore.

Unlike some of our other books, which are dated, this is more of a dip-in-and-out guide that you can open up as and when you wish to pick one thing to focus on for that day. As with all my writings and musings, I put myself into the story and questioned my own behaviours, penning a few of my own shortfalls and lessons. This book includes lots of resources that my whole team has contributed to – whether in the form of an app, a book, a podcast or a brand – so that if it's a tip or a topic you want to dive into, there is something within easy reach to help you do a bit more of your own research. We understand that due to the nature of business, all of the resources listed may not be around forever (although we hope they are!) they are correct, alive and well at the time of printing. If you know of any great resources that could be added in please DM us @collectivehub and we'll be sure to update in our next edition!

This is not a book to make you feel bad or less than. But rather, this is a book of little prompts and ideas for those of us wondering how we can do better, be better and work together to make a change for the country, environment and land that we live in and love.

Lisa and the Collective Hub team xo

contents

JANUARY
ETHICAL LIVING ——————————————— 6

FEBRUARY
ANIMAL FRIENDLY ——————————————— 38

MARCH
FOOD WASTE ——————————————— 68

APRIL
HEALTH, WELLNESS
AND BEAUTY ——————————————— 100

MAY
SUSTAINABILITY ——————————————— 132

JUNE
SHOPPING ——————————————— 166

JULY
RANDOM ACTS
OF KINDNESS ——————————————— 198

AUGUST
SELF-LOVE _____ 228

SEPTEMBER
TRAVEL _____ 260

OCTOBER
ENTERTAINING
AND CHRISTMAS _____ 292

NOVEMBER
SUSTAINABLE CAUSES
TO SUPPORT _____ 324

DECEMBER
GLOBAL CHARITIES THAT
NEED RELIEF _____ 350

ABOUT
LISA MESSENGER _____ 372

+ EXTRAS _____ 375

january
ethical living

Ethical living is as broad a topic as it is a varied one, and it's a matter that has long been close to my heart. While it would be almost impossible (not to mention time-consuming and costly) to live an entirely ethical existence, there are tweaks and refinements we can make to our current lifestyle habits that will subsequently do good for the planet, the environment and the people and places around us. Whether you take just one of these tips on board or 20, know that any change – however small it may seem – has the ability to make a difference.

BE FASHION CONSCIOUS

my musing

For most of the time I'm a yoga-tights-and-sports-bra kinda girl, but when I'm in the public eye, I do like donning an occasional pretty dress. With the rise in fast fashion, I love how many brands are owning their accountability, and ensuring their offering is an ethical one.

resource: read

The Conscious Closet: The Revolutionary Guide to Looking Good While Doing Good by Elizabeth L Cline.

pick - up - trash

my musing

This is something I try to do daily. It's so easy to walk past litter on the footpath, but do a good deed for the day and pick up someone else's trash. I'm often surprised how many people just step over it. We've all gotta live in this world so let's do our bit.

resource: register

Head to cleanup.org.au and register to create or join a clean-up event. Remember to invite your friends!

Turn off lights and *unplug* electrical equipment

my musing

We're all guilty of not doing this all the time, but try to make a habit of it, and you'll be surprised at how second nature it becomes. I rather fill my home with eco-friendly beeswax candles for ambient lighting.

resource: **mark in your cal**

Make Earth Hour (earthhour.org.au) an annual event in your diary.

BUY A REUSABLE WATER BOTTLE

my musing

With so many gorgeous options on the market these days, there really is no excuse not to. I also use charcoal in my water bottles to help purify, rather than buying off the shelf.

resource: buy

I love S'well stainless steel water bottles (swell.com).

produce less waste

my musing

There are so many ways to do this, and often it really is as simply as being more conscious and intentional in your day-to-day habits, to see where you can easily cut down on waste.

resource: **learn**

The 1 Million Women site has lots of tips on reducing your waste (1millionwomen.com.au).

Buy a reusable coffee cup

my musing

Gone are the days when reusable coffee cups were hard to come by, and with so many beautiful hand-painted options there's no longer any good reason not to have at least two in your arsenal.

resource: buy

One of my favourite brands is Pottery For The Planet (potteryfortheplanet.com).

QUESTION WHERE YOUR CLOTHES COME FROM

my musing

Something we should all take heed of. Let's move away from fast fashion and opt for ethically made pieces instead. Think quality over quantity.

resource: watch

Watch *The True Cost* on Netflix.

DON'T BE SHY ABOUT WHAT YOU BELIEVE IN

my musing

Share your opinion with friends, contact brands that should do better and be vocal in your beliefs. We all have a voice, make sure yours is heard.

resource: follow the link

https://www.theodysseyonline.com/10-tips-stand-what-believe

Shop second-hand

my musing

You never know what you might find at your local flea market or op-shop. Some of my fave pieces I've worn on red carpets have been one-off op-shop finds.

resource: read

Clothing Poverty: The Hidden World of Fast Fashion and Second-Hand Clothes by Andrew Brooks.

Invest in energy-saving equipment

my musing

A smart charging station is an essential bit of technology for most modern homes. I love having a charging dock where I can stick all my devices that need charging, without having to worry about turning it off.

resource: take a look

Try a smart charging station that stops charging and shuts down the adapter once the battery is full. You'll find a wide range on Amazon (amazon.com.au).

stick to the speed limit

my musing

Glaringly obvious yet still something we all need to pay more attention to; if you choose to drive, do your safety and the environment some good by sticking to the speed limit. Faster speeds increase harmful emissions that contribute to air pollution.

resource: check

Remember to check your speedometer regularly! If you have the latest version of Google Maps, it'll also show what speed you're supposed to be going.

my musing

Go old school with some stylish layers and cosy knits instead of reaching for the thermostat. Your heating bill, and the planet, will thank you for it.

resource: **rug up**

I love Melbourne brand Uimi for cosy knitwear (uimi.com.au).

my musing

While they may be a traditional romantic gesture, flowers have their own carbon footprint to contend with, so get creative when it comes to gifting that special someone in your life. Or give a living plant – those of you who know me will know this is almost my fave type of gift to give and receive.

resource: read

Why not send a package from Australian brand The Goods Tube? They offer beautiful products selected by style gurus from around the world, all packaged in a recycled cardboard tube (thegoodstube.com).

Eco-luxe
your bathroom

my musing

I recently reno'd my bathroom, and I always try to take into account ways that I can make any home improvements without impacting the environment. From upcycled materials to second-hand sinks, think outside the box and you'll be surprised at how easy eco-luxe can be.

resource: check out

Improve your carbon footprint by opting for solar-powered lighting and hot water systems. You may also want to consider a low-flow showerhead, which will help save water.

DRINK GREEN TEA

my musing

When it comes to tea, there are so many brands to choose from, so it's important to pay attention to where you put your coin, and buy from conscious companies.

resource: buy

Try Arbor Teas, which are organic and Fairtrade-certified and come in compostable packaging. Organic Matcha Maiden is another of my faves. Check them out on Insta @matcha_maiden.

PURCHASE AS MANY FAIRTRADE ITEMS AS POSSIBLE

my musing

While they used to be trickier to come by, Fairtrade items are much more widely available these days, and it means that intentional, ethical shopping is more accessible to everyone.

resource: visit

Head to fairtrade.com.au to find out more.

Ride public transport as often as you can

my musing

Hop on a bus, or enjoy a long train journey with nothing but a good book and the rolling hills in the distance for pleasure. I have to be honest, I pretty much never do this, but I do try to walk as much as I can – great for me and great for the environment.

resource: **head to**

https://www.switchyourthinking.com/ways-to-switch/transport

Take leftovers *home* from a restaurant

my musing

Yes to this – always, and unashamedly. The only other place it's ever going is the bin. Some waitstaff are funny about this due to regulatory concerns about food poisoning, but do it wherever you can.

resource: invest

I love my stainless steel Nesting Containers from Ever Eco for this (evereco.com.au).

Buy a meal for a homeless person

my musing
A simple act of goodwill can make all the difference to the day of someone less fortunate than ourselves.

resource: **do good**
Check out Foodbank.org.au – I recently became an ambassador. They service more than 2400 charities and 2000 schools Australia wide. The statistics are staggering.

my musing

Now that it's more accessible, and affordable, than ever before, if you're in a position to do so, always opt for organic. It's better for our health and the planet.

resource: i love

The Source Bulk Foods is one of my go-tos for organic food (thesourcebulkfoods.com.au). Take your own container and cut down on waste too!

GIVE BACK

my musing
One of the most rewarding things we can do in life, and a great reminder of how much we have, is to make giving back a consistent habit, whatever it looks like to you.

resource: give
Volunteer Match can connect you with a cause that you're passionate about (volunteermatch.org).

make DIY cleaning products

my musing

If you've got a bit of extra time on your hands, making your own cleaning products is a great way of reducing waste. White vinegar is something most of us have at home, and if you mix one part with two parts water you can use it to clean surfaces, sinks and stubborn stains. Try adding a squeeze of lemon or a few drops of your favourite essential oils for a fresh fragrance.

resource: jump online

A quick search on YouTube will give you lots of tips and tricks for doing it yourself at home.

OFFSET YOUR CARBON EMISSION WITH A VOLUNTARY CARBON TAX

my musing

Something I always try to do when I fly; it's a simple step for the frequent travellers among us – and often less expensive than you might think. The tax is invested in sustainable energy projects that help reduce CO_2 emissions at a faster rate.

resource: follow the link

Want to learn more? Head to carbonfootprint.com to find out all about this.

MOVE YOUR MONEY INTO AN *ETHICAL* BANK OR BUILDING SOCIETY

my musing

With more awareness around the idea of 'green banking', investigate who you bank with. Find out what they are using your money for – and if their morals and ethics aren't aligned with yours, make yourself heard by moving banks.

resource: go online

Bank Australia is a pioneer in green banking (bankaust.com.au).

Avoid plastic wherever possible

my musing

Reusable coffee cups and water bottles, soap instead of shower gel, loose fruit and veg from the grocery store – whatever it looks like to you, commit to using as little plastic as you can.

resource: plug in

Listen to The Mindbodygreen Podcast. Bonnie Wright's 5 Simple Tips to Reduce Plastic Today is an inspiring episode.

Use a water-saving flush cistern

my musing

A simple, one-off purchase that really can make the world of difference. I don't yet have one of these but it's on my radar.

resource: go online

Grohe has a great range of concealed cisterns that are designed to save water (grohe.com.au).

Buy ethical jewellery

my musing

Gone are the days when ethically made jewellery was hard to come by, and with so many stunning options on offer it's an easy switch, without compromising on style.

resource: peruse

https://goodonyou.eco/the-ultimate-guide-to-ethical-jewellery

COLLECT RAINWATER FOR PLANTS AND ANIMALS

my musing

I love this idea, and it's such an easy thing for all of us to do. It not only preserves water, but it also looks after much-needed flora and fauna as well. I'm well known for putting containers out for animals to drink from, wherever I am in the world.

resource: collect

Head to your local Bunnings store to pick up a rainwater tank.

Invest in consciously made furniture

my musing

Next time you're upgrading your interiors, if you can afford to, invest in something that will last. Flat-pack furniture often has a limited shelf life and ends up in landfill. Also look at furniture made from sustainably sourced materials.

resource: invest

West Elm has a great stock of sustainable & FSC®-certified furniture (westelm.com.au).
Head to au.fsc.org to learn more about sustainable furniture.

Buy *organic* bedding

my musing

There's nothing better than beautiful, buttery bedlinen, and you'll no doubt notice a huge difference to your shut-eye if your bedding is organic.

resource: **sleep tight**

I love the 100% French flax linen bedding from Bed Threads (bedthreads.com.au). Eadie Lifestyle is also a favourite (eadielifestyle.com.au).

Do your research and stay informed

my musing
Stay curious; keep learning and always question. Educating ourselves is not only free, it's essential if we want change to happen.

resource: watch
Watch Netflix documentary *Minimalism* by The Minimalists.

february
animal friendly

Most of us love our furry friends, yet there is still something of a disparity between our adoration for animals and our willingness to consume animal products – whatever form they come in. Whether this is the year you pledge to go meat-free on Mondays, or you decide to give up leather for good, here are some ways all of us can start prioritising the welfare of animals above our own consumer desires.

GO
VEGAN

my musing

With mounting evidence that eating meat carries with it a huge impact on the planet, if veganism is an option for you, there's never been a better time to embrace a plant-based diet.

resource: read

Veganomicon: The Ultimate Vegan Cookbook by Isa Chandra Moskowitz and Terry Hope Romero is full of delicious vegan recipes to inspire you.

If you can't go vegan, go *vegetarian*

my musing

These tips are about what works for you, and if going vegan isn't something you can, or want, to do, but vegetarianism is, opt for that instead. I'd say I'm about 95 per cent vegetarian, just as an FYI.

resource: **tune in**

Listen to VegCast: The Vegetarian Podcast.

IF YOU CAN'T GO VEGETARIAN, CONSIDER BECOMING A PESCATARIAN

my musing

Going pescatarian is a much more realistic option for many of us, so if this feels right for you, why not explore a fish-only diet?

resource: read

Pescetarian Kitchen Food Blog is a great resource for recipes.

IF YOU DON'T WANT TO CUT OUT MEAT COMPLETELY TRY A MEAT-FREE MONDAY

my musing

Even opting to go meat-free once a week will have a positive impact on the planet; so if this fits best with you when it comes to consuming animal products, know that even a small tweak like this can do the world of good when we do it collectively.

resource: get inspired

Take a look at meatfreemondays.com for ideas.

Learn your protein sources

my musing

It's a common misconception that meat is the best source of protein. Do your research, read blogs, buy plant-based recipe books and get to know the beans, vegetables and pulses that are most conducive to a high-protein diet.

resource: get educated

The Mindbodygreen website offers some credible info on the protein-rich vegetables you should be filling up on (mindbodygreen.com).

Eat compassionately

my musing

Whether you go vegan, schedule meat-free Mondays or simply decide to buy free-range eggs or source meat from your local butcher, get into the habit of being deliberate and compassionate in your eating choices.

resource: **read**

The Ethical Carnivore: My Year Killing to Eat by Louise Gray.

PLEDGE TO GO FUR-FREE

my musing

With so many stylish faux-fur fashion and homeware options available these days, going fur-free is an easy pledge to make.

resource: find fur-free brands

Coach is just one brand that has adopted a 100 per cent fur-free policy (coachaustralia.com).

Don't buy leather

my musing

While in days gone by synthetic alternatives were anything but stylish, with brands like Stella McCartney leading the way with sustainable vegetarian leather, avoiding real leather is an easy and fashion-conscious decision for many of us.

resource: research

Stella McCartney has a beautiful range of vegetarian leather, and watch this space for lab-grown leather too.

Think twice about eggs

my musing

A nutritious breakfast staple for many of us, it's important that we are aware of the process that goes into the production of the eggs we're eating. Educate yourself on where your eggs come from, and if you're not happy, source a farmers' market or similar where you know the livestock is treated with compassion and kindness. When you're buying free-range eggs, look for the 'stocking density' printed on egg cartons; the fewer hens per hectare the better.

resource: get educated

Australianeggs.org.au offers lots of information on buying eggs from happy hens, and how to avoid misleading claims.

reconsider dairy

my musing

I'm not here to preach, or tell you what you should and shouldn't be eating (or drinking) – I'm by no means perfect. Having said that, there is mounting evidence that the production of dairy can be traumatic for the animals involved. If eliminating – or lessening – your dairy intake is an option for you, there are many plant-based alternatives you can consider such as oat, almond, soy, macadamia and coconut milk.

resource: watch

'Dairy is Scary' by Canadian vegan activist Erin Janus on YouTube.

DON'T SUPPORT ANIMAL ENTERTAINMENT

my musing

A simple form of entertainment for all of us to avoid. Make your opinion known by where you do (and don't) spend your money. There are still circuses that use animals in Australia, unlike many other countries where the practice is banned.

resource: be aware

Want to know why we should call for a ban? Head here: https://www.rspca.org.au/blog/2017/truth-about-exotic-animals-circuses

Buy cruelty-free beauty products

my musing

With more and more beauty brands pledging to go cruelty-free, there's never been a better time to rethink your beauty regimen.

resource: **buy right**

PETA's website has a comprehensive list of cruelty-free beauty brands (peta.org.au).

KNOWLEDGE IS POWER – DO YOUR RESEARCH BEFORE YOU SHOP

my musing

We only know what we know, so before buying your next moisturiser or serum, do your research and be aware of where you're spending your money. Many companies have stopped testing on animals – however, we still have a long way to go.

resource: follow the link

Head to One Green Planet's website for tips on researching your purchases (onegreenplanet.org).

VOLUNTEER AT YOUR LOCAL ANIMAL SHELTER

my musing

If you're in a position where you can donate a day a month to a local animal shelter, you'll feel all the better for spending time with our furry friends.

resource: make some time

The RSPCA is a great place to start (rspca.org.au).

adopt a dog from a rescue centre

my musing

If you're considering getting a dog, buying one from a rescue home will make the world of difference to a pet pooch who may well have been ill-treated by its previous owner.

resource: jump online

Petrescue.com.au can help you find a dog in need of a home in your area.

Avoid buying silk

my musing

Once seen as one of the most luxurious fabrics around, silk is not without its animal issues – in particular, the way silk worms are killed. Do your research and decide whether or not you're comfortable wearing silk.

resource: **research brands**

Some brands, such as ASOS, refuse to sell silk as part of a ban on a host of animal-derived materials. You can read more on the ethical issues here: https://qz.com/quartzy/1309227/asos/is-banning-silk-but-is-it-really-unethical-to-wear

Consider fostering animals

my musing

If you love animals, but aren't in a position to care for one full-time, look into fostering pets as a great alternative.

resource: give a home

Rspca.org.au and petrescue.com.au are great resources for anyone wanting to foster pets.

HAVE YOUR ANIMAL DESEXED

my musing

This is a simple way to avoid unwanted pets that all dog and cat owners should consider. The fewer unwanted pets, the fewer animals there are in shelters.

resource: book an appointment

Discuss getting your pet desexed with your local vet. Generally it's kinder to have animals desexed at a younger age, as the procedure is simple and the recovery rapid.

Read the labels

my musing
Such a simple thing to do, but if you get into the habit of reading labels before you buy anything, the power of going cruelty-free is entirely in your hands.

resource: download
Check out the Cruelty-Free app by Leaping Bunny, which allows you to search by product type and company name, or scan a product's UPC code.

Boycott Brands That Test on animals

my musing

Be vocal. Tell your favourite brands why you're boycotting them and demand that they do better.

resource: learn

Animalsaustralia.org has a wealth of info about animal testing, and how you can not only avoid products tested on animals, but also other ways you can make a difference.

UNDERSTAND CONFUSING INGREDIENTS

my musing

If you're not familiar with the ingredients in the products that you purchase, do your homework and make more informed choices. Often the key to doing better is knowing more. It's as simple as that.

resource: follow the link

https://ethicalelephant.com/cruelty-free-vegan-labels-logos

KNOW WHAT
TO AVOID

my musing
It's only by becoming familiar with what, and who, tests on animals that we will know what to avoid as shoppers.

resource: check it out
For a list of the brands that still test on animals head here: https://www.animalsaustralia.org/features/animal-testing-list.php

Download an app

my musing

In the age of technology in which we live, we have a fountain of knowledge and know-how at our fingertips. Something as simple as having an app on your phone can give us the understanding we need to make better decisions.

resource: download

Bunny Free by PETA is a great go-to app.

Avoid microbeads

my musing

Given their hugely damaging effect on marine life, beauty products containing microbeads (those small, solid particles that you might find in your exfoliator or face wash) are something we should all avoid if we can.

resource: **throw the beads out**

Beat The Microbead by Plastic Soup Foundation is a fab campaign that compiles lists of products containing microbeads for numerous countries around the world (beatthemicrobead.org).

IF YOU WANT TO BUY WOOL, BUY IT ETHICALLY

my musing

With so many brands now selling ethical wool, there's no excuse not to. Despite high standards in Australia, not all wool is created without causing harm to sheep.

resource: jump online

A brand I love is Eco Mono (ecomono.com.au). You can read more about ethical wool at

https://goodonyou.eco/material-guide-ethical-wool

MAKE YOUR GARDEN BEE-FRIENDLY

my musing

Not all of us have backyards, but if you're one of the lucky few, making yours bee-friendly is a great way to look after this species. And we all know by now what the consequences of a bee-free planet would be for the human race.

resource: plant!

Visit aussiebee.com.au for tips and tricks on avoiding insecticides, how to make a bee hotel, and selecting plants that flower year-round.

Buy alpaca products

my musing

Alpacas literally have to be happy in order to create good fibres. A cosy jumper and the knowledge that the material has come from a happy alpaca – what could be better?

resource: read

A lot of the alpaca knitwear available is blended with merino wool and man-made fibres. Look for a higher percentage of alpaca wool, and be prepared to pay for quality.

Seek out eco-friendly leather

my musing

I love scouring the internet for ethical brands. Get into the habit of doing your research before you commit to a new purchase.

resource: **jump online**

Check out brands Happy Genie (happy-genie.com) and Veggani (veggani.com) ,who use apple leather to make chic handbags.

"Not responding
is a response -
we are equally
responsible for
what we don't do."

– Jonathan Safran Foer

march food waste

Unnecessary food waste happens to the best of us. Yet, whatever we're currently doing (or not doing) to eliminate needless waste, there is no doubt more that can be done. I know that I'm guilty of letting food go off in the fridge, over-calculating portion sizes, and mindless food shopping – all of which are habits I'm determined to break this year. None of us are perfect, and it would be ambitious for anyone to attempt all of the tips I've outlined here for minimising food waste, but if each of us takes just a couple of them on board, a change can, and will, start to come. One of the single best overarching resources to support this chapter is Foodbank.org

buy less

my musing
Simple, but oh-so effective.

resource: read
Food Choice and Sustainability: Why Buying Local, Eating Less Meat, and Taking Baby Steps Won't Work by Richard Oppenander.

Plan meals in advance

my musing
An easy thing for most of us to do, and something that almost guarantees eliminating food waste.

resource: get creative
Look up https://savethefood.com/articles/10-easy-tips-for-meal-planning for savvy ways to work every last ingredient into tasty dishes.

USE A DELIVERY SERVICE

my musing

If you're time poor, an ethical delivery service can make last-minute grocery shopping a thing of the past. Try Hello Fresh or Marley Spoon, who only deliver the portions you need and focus on recycling or reusing their packaging.

resource: sign up

Hellofresh.com.au; marleyspoon.com.au; aussiefarmers.com.au

EAT LEFTOVERS

my musing

Get into the habit of turning leftovers into meals. It's not only a good way to keep your grocery bill down, but it's also good for cutting back on food waste.

resource: cook

Jamieoliver.com has some imaginative recipes for whipping up an impressive meal with your leftovers.

understand expiration dates

my musing

Many of us fall into the habit of binning anything that's passed its best-before date, but it's important to know that these are simply guidelines, and some foods are edible way beyond their alleged shelf life. Note: 'Best-before' is not to be confused with 'use-by'; foods pose a health or safety risk if eaten after their use-by dates.

resource: check out

Foodstandards.gov.au is my go-to resource for food-expiry information.

Shop smart

my musing

Be more considered and calculated when you do your weekly shop to avoid overspending and buying foods you simply don't need. Always write a shopping list before you go, and stick to it – and don't forget your reusable bags!

resource: plan

Bookmark foodwise.com.au and use it for smart shopping tips.

BUY FUNNY-LOOKING VEGETABLES

my musing

I love my local Harris Farm's misshapen vegetables; they don't come in plastic packaging and are just as tasty as their perfect-looking alternatives.

resource: check out

Try Harris Farm's Imperfect Picks. You can also head to your local farmers' market for fresh, seasonal and often organic fruit and veg.

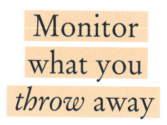

Monitor what you *throw* away

my musing

Only by assessing exactly what foods you're throwing away can you gain a better idea of how much you're wasting, so you can make a conscious decision to do better in future.

resource: learn

Mashable.com has some informative food waste tips (https://mashable.com/2015/02/15/food-waste-tips/).

Designate one dinner a week as a use-it-up meal

my musing

I love getting creative in the kitchen with leftovers. Make it a weekly thing and you'll soon add to your repertoire of recipes.

resource: jump online

Simplyrecipes.com has a great collection of use-it-up-meal recipes

REPURPOSE SCRAP FOOD

my musing

Whatever this looks like to you – whether a salad made of odds and ends or a tray of roasted scrap vegetables – make binning scrap food a thing of the past.

resource: watch

Check out Sweet Potato Soul's video 'Life Changing Food Scrap Recipes' by Jenné Claiborne for some genius tips.

Compost

my musing

Even after using up scraps and leftovers, you're still going to end up with some waste. Composting is an easy and inexpensive way to reduce your carbon footprint. You can either invest in a composting system yourself or check if your council or organisations in your area will collect your food scraps for composting initiatives.

resource: get some tips

Gardeningknowhow.com has some excellent tips for first-time composters.

DONATE
UNWANTED
FOOD

my musing

If you find yourself with food you won't get around to eating, donating it to your local soup kitchen or homeless shelter is a wonderful way of paying it forward.

resource: donate

Head to foodbank.org.au for more information on how, what and where to donate.

Avoid temptation when shopping

my musing

Make a list and stick to it. It's a simple strategy to utilise to avoid food waste.

resource: check out

The AnyList app is a great way to do this, and you can share your lists with others too.

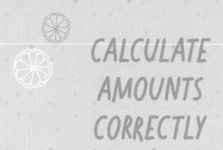

CALCULATE AMOUNTS CORRECTLY

my musing
Something you'll get the hang of the more you cook. Avoid using more than you need to eliminate the chances of making food that will go to waste.

resource: calculate
Lovefoodhatewaste.com has a handy Portion Calculator.

store food properly

my musing
Something as simple as storing your food correctly can give it a longer shelf life, thus avoiding the likelihood of things going off sooner than they should.

resource: pin!
Pinterest has a heap of ideas for stylish food storage – whatever your budget.

meal prep

my musing

I love setting aside time on a Sunday to meal prep for the week ahead. Make it part of your weekly routine and you'll be amazed at how easy it will become to reduce food waste.

resource: prep!

Delish.com is a useful resource for meal-prepping tips and tricks.

Don't over serve food

my musing
One of my mantras when it comes to serving is that you can always add, but you can't take away!

resource: smaller
Invest in portion-control plates for an easy way to avoid over serving.

TRY CANNING AND PICKLING

my musing

A custom more associated with older generations, canning and pickling is becoming more and more mainstream. It can make food last up to an incredible five years, not to mention elevating any meal.

resource: jump online

Eatingwell.com has a comprehensive guide to pickling for beginners. Also, read *Grown & Gathered* by Matt & Lentil.

Use *helpful* apps

my musing

There's an app for almost everything these days, so if food waste is something you want to address, download an app that will help you with your endeavours.

resource: download

The OLIO app helps to connect neighbours and local retailers so surplus food can be shared rather than disposed of.

Learn to preserve

my musing

Food preservation can be used to not only keep food for longer but also to reduce waste, save money and enjoy local and seasonal produce year-round – and yummy too (think jams, chutneys, relishes).

resource: read

Read *The Modern Preserver* by Kylee Newton.

EAT
THE
SKIN

my musing

There are ample benefits to eating the skin of foods. Often it's the most nutrient-dense part of a fruit or vegetable.

resource: jump online

A quick online search will tell you which skins to eat and cook with, and which to avoid.

Ditch
coffee pods
and tea bags

my musing

We all love our morning caffeine fix, but be intentional in how you consume it. Buy ground coffee (even better, grind your own) and loose leaf tea to reduce waste, not to mention make a far superior brew!

resource: change

Thegoodtrade.com features an inclusive list of some of the best Fairtrade coffee brands around.

Swap plastic lunch boxes for ethical alternatives

my musing

I love stainless steel lunch boxes and food storage containers as a sustainable way to store my food. Glass and bamboo are other alternatives too.

resource: **check it out**

EKOBO is a premium range of bamboo fibre accessories that I love (by-ekobo.com).

BUY A STAINLESS STEEL STRAW

my musing

We all know that plastic straws end up in the ocean. Choose not to be part of the problem by investing in reusable straws.

resource: change

Sip Well is one of the best stainless steel straw brands on the market.

Use wax wraps *instead* of cling wrap

my musing

With wax wraps so readily available now, it's an easy and relatively inexpensive swap to make. You can even have a go at making your own beeswax wraps if you're game.

resource: check it out

I like Beeswax Wraps Australia.

https://beeswaxwraps.com.au/

Make your own milk and butter alternatives

my musing

Get creative in the kitchen by trying out homemade dairy alternatives.

resource: make your own

Simpleveganblog.com has lots of plant-based milk recipes to try.

BUY LOCAL AND SEASONAL GROCERIES

my musing

Buying local and seasonal is an easy way to ensure your grocery shopping has as low a carbon footprint as possible.

resource: read

In Season: Cooking With Vegetables and Fruit by Sarah Raven.

look **out** for **farmers' markets**
or allotments **where** you
can **buy** produce **that** was
grown locally **and** didn't
travel **far** to **get** to **you**

my musing

I love my local farmers' market in Bondi. If there's one near you, make it a place you do your weekly grocery shop.

resource: plant!

Find a market near you at farmersmarkets.org.au

IF YOU LIKE FIZZY DRINKS, BUY A SODA STREAM TO MAKE YOUR OWN

my musing
Going retro in the kitchen with a Soda Stream is another way to cut back on your plastic waste.

resource: read
Go to sodastream.com.au to check out the range. Plus, they've introduced an organic range, including a kombucha syrup.

Search for *local* breweries and wineries that offer *refills*

my musing

If you love a daily tipple of wine, finding a winery or bottle shop that offers refills is one way of avoiding unnecessary rubbish. Or give up drinking altogether like I have… but that's another story!

resource: **search**

Seek out stores and wineries with refillable beer and wine stations in your area – they're popping up everywhere.

Make your own cordials

my musing

I love a homemade cordial; they're usually tastier than the shop-bought alternatives, and are a great way to drink your favourite flavour guilt-free – not to mention a nifty way to use up any fruit peelings, too.

resource: follow the steps

Bestrecipes.com.au has a step-by-step guide on how to do it.

health, wellness and beauty

april

While I've never been the type of person who spends hours on their beauty routine, it's suffice to say it's an industry responsible for an alarming amount of waste – regardless of how simplified our morning routines are. From shaving to shampoo, there are so many ways we can reduce our waste – some of which may not have occurred to you before. And so, for April, I've rounded up some simple swaps that you can easily incorporate into your lifestyle to help lessen your waste, without compromising on looking (or feeling) your best.

SWAP TAMPONS FOR A MENSTRUAL CUP

my musing

While menstrual cups have only been around for a few years, they're becoming more and more mainstream, and certainly go a long way to reducing coastal clutter.

resource: try

Check out one of our favourite friends startups @wearescarlet (scarletperiod.com) for all things periods and menstrual cups!

INVEST IN A STAINLESS STEEL SAFETY RAZOR

my musing

So many shopping habits are ingrained in us that we don't even consider environmental alternatives. Personally, disposable razors were something I didn't think twice about buying, but knowing that a stainless steel razor lasts so much longer, it's a simple switch to make.

resource: **invest**

Biome.com.au have a brilliant selection.

BUY TOILET PAPER AND TISSUES THAT ARE PACKAGED IN RECYCLED/BAMBOO PAPER

my musing

Recycled toilet paper is a really easy swap to make when you're doing your weekly household shop.

resource: check out

Who Gives A Crap is my go-to brand (au. whogivesacrap.org). The paper is 100 per cent recycled, and 50 per cent of profits are donated to build toilets in the developing world.

Use a bamboo toothbrush

my musing

Bamboo alternatives are no longer available only online and at health stores, you can pick them up at pharmacies and supermarkets now too, so there's no excuse to choose plastic anymore.

resource: swap

Flora & Fauna stock a good selection of inexpensive bamboo brushes (floraandfauna.com.au).

Switch your bottled shampoo to a shampoo bar

my musing

A brilliant substitute for bottled shampoo, bars do the job just as well and are a whole lot less harmful to the environment.

resource: check out

Lush have myriad shampoo bar offerings available (au.lush.com).

Swap shower gel for soap

my musing

Another easy replacement to make, bars of soap not only produce less waste, they're often less pricey than their shower gel counterpart, and tend to last longer.

resource: try

I love Kiehl's for soap bars (kiehls.com.au).

RECYCLE EMPTY MAKE-UP CONTAINERS

my musing

It's all-too-easy to just chuck empty bottles away, so get into the practice of recycling them as soon as you've finished with them.

resource: **check out**

1millionwomen.com.au has a lot of helpful tips!

Find a plastic-free dental floss

my musing

Something I had never considered until I looked into ways in which to cut down on my waste. There are sustainable alternatives for almost anything if you look hard enough.

resource: make the switch

Florandfauna.com.au sells plant-based dental floss.

AVOID USING FACE WIPES

my musing

A serious offender for surplus waste, face-wipes are not only pretty bad for your skin (ask any beauty expert and they'll verify this), they're also bad for the environment.

resource: try this!

Try using micellar water (available at most supermarkets and pharmacies) and a cotton face washer.

Replace your plastic cotton buds with *wood-stemmed* ones

my musing

If you can't go without cotton buds, make the ones you use as sustainable as possible.

resource: try

Hydrophil Bamboo Cotton Swabs are made from biodegradable bamboo stems and soft certified organic cotton.

USE APPLE CIDER VINEGAR

my musing

Almost everyone has a bottle of apple cider vinegar lying around the house, and it has a whole host of beauty benefits – from minimising pores to helping with overly oily skin.

resource: **give it a go**

Easily bought from your local supermarket or health food store. Look for raw, organic and unfiltered brands with 'the mother' included.

CHOOSE A SUSTAINABLE SALON FOR YOUR HAIRCUTS

my musing

Next time you need a haircut or colour, find a nearby salon whose ethics align with your own.

resource: follow the link!

Sustainablesalons.org

Raid your kitchen for homemade beauty products

my musing

You'll be surprised what you have lying around your kitchen that can double up as a beauty product – everything from honey to yoghurt.

resource: download

YouTube has some brilliant step-by-step guides for DIY beauty products.

BUY A SOAP NUT – A COMPOSTABLE ALTERNATIVE TO LAUNDRY POWDERS AND LIQUIDS

my musing

Much more environmentally friendly than individually wrapped detergents, soap nuts last longer and are easily compostable.

resource: check out

I love That Red House Organic Soapberries (thatredhouse.com.au). And also The Dirt Company (thedirtcompany.com.au).

Look for products containing *botanical marine* extracts and algae

my musing

Good for your skin and great for the environment – it's a win-win situation.

resource: look out for...

Skyn Iceland is a vegan and cruelty-free natural skin-care range that uses algae in its products (skyniceland.com).

Eliminate microplastics

my musing

With the growing awareness around the damage microplastics cause to our wildlife, it's best to avoid products that include them as an ingredient.

resource: say goodbye

Visit environment.gov.au for more information on why this is so important.

Replace petroleum derivatives with ingredients such as *beeswax, cocoa butter* and *vegetable oils*

my musing

Moving towards a more natural-based skincare regimen will do wonders for your skin, without having a harmful effect on the planet.

resource: check out

Earth Tu Face Face Balm is one of my teams favourite beeswax beauty products (earthtuface.com).

Seek make-up brushes made from bamboo

my musing

This is a switch I made a while ago. I love bamboo products and find that, because they're a natural fibre, they're much kinder to my skin.

resource: try

Nourishedlife.com.au has a fab Bamboo Vegan Makeup Brush Set by Life Basics.

OPT FOR MULTIPURPOSE PRODUCTS

my musing

My team loves a good multipurpose product; they're cost-effective, save on space, and are +- far less likely to cause excess waste.

resource: go multi!

Try something like Make's Dew Pot in Lily, which adds a pop of luminous pink to lids, lips and cheeks.

Simplify your *skincare* routine

my musing

I've always had a very straightforward skincare routine, and there are so many benefits to simplifying yours. It will most likely save you both time and money, and the fewer products you use, the less waste you'll produce.

resource: simplify!

Try using just an antioxidant serum and a good quality moisturiser with a minimum SPF of 30.

Be mindful of how much you use

my musing

It's all too easy to overuse products, such as shampoo and conditioner, meaning you'll be replacing them at a far quicker rate than need be. Be mindful of how much you're using and you'll be surprised at how much longer things last.

resource: **jump online**

A pea-sized amount of most cosmetics should be more than enough, and a squirt of shampoo should be roughly the size of a cherry or raspberry, depending on your hair length. And only apply conditioner to the ends of your hair.

USE BRANDS THAT HAVE RECYCLING PROGRAMS

my musing

More and more brands are cottoning on to the fact that their consumers are becoming more mindful of where they spend their money. Seek out companies that do their bit for the environment with a recycling scheme.

resource: **give back**

Australian brands that offer a recycling rewards scheme currently include Kiehl's, MAC, Lush, Jurlique, The Body Shop and some Le Labo stores, to name a few.

- -

Understand
the four pillars
of sustainability

- -

my musing
No brand is perfect, but by ensuring the ones you use adhere to at least one arm of sustainability, you can purchase their products with your mind at ease.

resource: get the info!
Futurelearn.com has more information on this, which is well worth a read.

Spread the word about green beauty products you love

♥

my musing

If there's a brand you love that's doing things right, shout about it! Tell your friends, post on social and do your bit to spread awareness.

resource: **share**

Nourished Life stock many trusted organic skincare brands (nourishedlife.com.au).

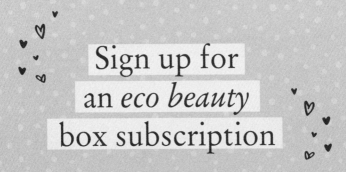

Sign up for an *eco beauty* box subscription

my musing

Eco beauty boxes are an easy way to put your money into brands who are doing their bit for the environment.

resource: sign up

My team are big fans of Organified Beauty Box (organifiedbeautybox.com.au).

PUT A RECYCLING BIN INSIDE YOUR BATHROOM

my musing
A simple yet effective way to ensure you're recycling everything you can.

resource: recycle
I love the Joseph Joseph Split 8 Waste & Recycling Bin, designed especially for sorting bathroom waste (josephjoseph.com).

buy in bulk

my musing

Just like groceries, buying cosmetics and toiletries in bulk is a great way to cut down on waste, and you'll probably save some money to boot!

resource: stock up

Biome Eco stores are great for purchasing beauty products in bulk. Head to biome.com.au to find your nearest store.

Avoid products that use *fancy packaging*, glosses and foils

my musing

Premium packaging might look nice, but if it's producing unnecessary waste that will harm the planet, opt for a greener alternative.

resource: **pick the packing**

L'Occitane uses recyclable packaging and offers refill pouches for many of their products, so that fewer containers are wasted. They also try to avoid outer packaging when possible.

SWITCH TO REUSABLE COTTON BALLS

my musing

I've certainly been guilty of throwing away cotton balls and pads in the past, with little or no thought to where they end up. By switching to reusable options you can minimise your personal waste.

resource: switch

Stock up on Amazon where you can buy reusable bamboo facial pads, or cotton pad alternatives. I like 'Jentl's 12 pack of reusable 100% bamboo cotton rounds, which come with a laundry bag (jentl.com.au).

MAKE
YOUR OWN
TOOTHPASTE

my musing

Fancy getting inventive in the bathroom? Making your own toothpaste is a good place to start. While it won't be for everyone, it's pretty simple to do and will save you some money too.

resource: watch

Head to YouTube for some comprehensive how-tos.

. . . .

"You have to hold yourself accountable for your actions, and that's how we're going to protect the Earth."

. . . .

– Jonathan Safran Foer

may
sustainability

In short, living sustainably, to me, means embracing a lifestyle that has as low an impact on the environment as it can, and living with as light a footprint as possible. There are so many ways we can do this – through diet, through daily habits, through consumption – and as with most things, there is always, always room for improvement. Having said that, I don't believe in self-flagellation for the things I can't, don't or, in some cases, won't do – but I do believe in doing what I can, when I can, to be as sustainable a person as possible. I hope these tips on sustainability will provide you with some food for thought, and some areas in which you can make small tweaks for the good of the planet.

SWITCH TO A GREEN ENERGY SUPPLIER

my musing

No one likes the faff of changing suppliers, but if doing so means you can help save the planet, it's a faff that's ultimately worth it.

resource: try

Powershop (powershop.com.au) and Diamond Energy (diamondenergy.com.au) both scored five stars in the Green Electricity Guide, so are great options if you want to go green.

Get a smart energy meter

my musing

A smart energy meter – a device that digitally measures your energy usage so you can keep track of it – is a worthy investment that will help conserve energy. All households should have one.

resource: **smarten up**

Reduction Revolution is one of the market leaders when it comes to smart meters (reductionrevolution.com.au).

Limit your screen time

my musing

Something I'm determined to cut down on this year! Screen time has so many drawbacks, including the sustainability side of it. Smart phone production, as well as the data centres that service every message, call and video, create an enormous amount of emissions.

resource: download

The Forest App is a fun and feel-good way to keep you off your phone. Check it out!

Keep an eye on your heating

my musing

It's all too easy to crank the heating up without a second thought when it's cold – and we all know that houses in Australia aren't exactly built for chillier climes. Be mindful of your heating, and opt for an extra cosy layer instead.

resource: **tip!**

Energy Made Easy has some practical tips on how to keep your heating down (energymadeeasy.gov.au).

BUY BAMBOO PAPER TOWELS

my musing

A simple switch to make around the house, but one that would have a notable effect on the planet if we all did it. Bamboo is a highly sustainable material, which requires no chemicals and little water to grow, plus it's biodegradable.

resource: switch

White Magic Reusable Bamboo Towels are my favourite.

BUY A WOODEN-HANDLED DISHWASHING BRUSH

my musing

Another simple transition to make in the kitchen, using wood or bamboo instead of plastic will soon become second nature to you if you do it often enough.

resource: **buy**

The Ecostore wooden dishwashing brush gets my vote (ecostore.com/au/).

Use a coconut or loofah-based scouring pad

my musing

When you're buying household items, always look a bit harder for a plant-based alternative – more often than not you'll find one.

resource: try

The Safix Scrub Pad is made from biodegradable coconut fibres and works a treat.

plant a *tree*

my musing

If you don't have a back garden in which to do it, there are many other ways you can get your hands dirty and plant a tree. A quick online search will give you a point in the right direction of how else you can do it.

resource: follow the link!

https://carbonneutral.com.au/plant-a-tree

my musing
When it comes to your fashion choices, be mindful of where the material has come from, and choose organic if you can.

resource: read up
The Guardian has a great online article about this:
https://www.theguardian.com/fashion/2019/oct/01/cotton-on-the-staggering-potential-of-switching-to-organic-clothes

USE LINEN AROUND THE HOME

my musing

A natural fibre and one with a low carbon footprint, linen is a great material to use around the home for that boho, beachy look. Organic linen is even better.

resource: **get the app**

Download the Good On You app to discover how your favourite brands measure up in the ethical stakes.

Replace cushion covers, towels, tablecloths and shower curtains with hemp alternatives

my musing
There are so many great hemp fabric options that are both stylish and kinder to the planet than their synthetic alternatives.

resource: check out
Madeinhemp.com.au has some seriously beautiful homewares available.

SEARCH FOR CEREALS THAT COME IN PAPER BAGS

my musing

While not an obvious choice, opting for cereals that come in paper bags rather than layers of plastic, makes an everyday essential a more ethical one.

resource: calculate

Look for brands such as Troo Granola, which comes in compostable packaging.

Make your own nut milk

my musing

Yes, it can be a bit time consuming and fiddly, but DIY nut milks are good for the gut, and even better for the planet.

resource: watch

YouTube is full of how-tos for homemade nut milk, also known as 'MYLK'.

Buy condiments and spreads in *glass* jars

my musing

Get into the practice of choosing glass packaging over plastic, and it will soon become an inherent part of your grocery shop.

resource: reduce waste!

Meridian sells everything from peanut butter to soy sauce in glass jars and bottles.

SWITCH TO AN ECO WATER BOTTLE

my musing

An absolute no-brainer. Buy yourself a reusable water bottle today.

resource: check out

Frank Green (frankgreen.com.au), Sol Cups (solcups. com) and S'Well (swell.com) are three of my favourite reusable water bottle brands.

REPLACE GLAD WRAP WITH WAX WRAP

my musing

Much like with the condemnation of plastic bags, I think (and hope) we're moving towards a time when wasteful plastics around the home will be a thing of the past.

resource: **reuse**

Bee Wrappy Beeswax Food Wraps are a sustainable and reusable alternative to single-use plastic (beewrappy.com.au).

Use reusable wrap instead of foil

my musing

A super easy switch to make, and one that will benefit the planet – and your purse strings.

resource: go silicone

Agreena 3 in1 Silicone Wrap is a practical alternative (agreena.world). It can replace cling wrap, aluminium foil and baking paper.

Replace plastic sandwich bags with biodegradable paper sandwich bags

my musing

Commit to no longer buying plastic sandwich bags, in the same way that you commit to always taking a shopper when you buy your groceries.

resource: try these!

Hercules Sustain compostable paper sandwich and snack resealable bags are an easy and inexpensive swap (sustainliving.com.au).

OPT FOR RECYCLED PAPER TOWELS

my musing

You can buy these as an alternative in most supermarkets. They are a little less absorbent but so much better for our world!

resource: **look out**

Look for packaging that states 'recycled' or 'green' and choose those instead.

GREEN CLEAN YOUR CLOTHES

my musing
Think before you put a wash on, and be mindful of the products you use.

resource: give these a go
Earthwise, Ecostore and Eco Planet are great green brands for cleaning clothes.

Use LED lightbulbs

my musing

There are so many benefits to switching to LED bulbs. Not only do they last for years, but they also draw substantially less power than older types of bulbs, plus they're less toxic as they don't contain mercury.

resource: try

Philips has a good range of these, and they are widely available.

BUY ENERGY-EFFICIENT APPLIANCES

my musing

Get into the habit of always investigating a product's sustainability before you say yes to the purchase. Look for the energy star rating when you buy new appliances. The more stars, the more efficient.

resource: jump online

1millionwomen.com has lots of accessible tips.

Wrap your water heater

my musing

An easy and inexpensive way to improve energy efficiency and save you money is to insulate your water heater, depending on the type of heater you have.

resource: research

Talk to your plumber about the type of heater you have and how you can keep it insulated. Energy.nsw. gov.au has a handy 'Hot Water Guide' which details different types of heaters and how you can save energy and water.

Seal draughts around the house

♥

my musing

Set aside a weekend to make your home as energy efficient as possible, and you'll reap the rewards for years to come. Putting up heavy curtains and using door snakes to keep out draughts is a good place to start.

resource: **search**

A quick internet search will show you how.

Consider travel *alternatives*

my musing

Get smart when it comes to travel; research, plan, and always consider sustainable alternatives if they're available to you.

resource: sign up!

The National Geographic website has lots of tips for sustainable travel (nationalgeographic.com).

Invest in a *shower timer*

my musing

I love a long shower but growing up in drought stricken country NSW, I try to be more of a get-in-and-get-out kind of girl, and a shower timer is a handy way of ensuring your morning shower is a sustainable one. Keep it under four minutes.

resource: get in time

There are many shower timers available, but any timing device will do!

PURCHASE BETTER QUALITY ITEMS THAT LAST LONGER

my musing

So much yes to this; I'm all about having fewer things of higher quality.

resource: go higher quality

Buy Me Once is a great website for sourcing high quality items, many of which are available in Australia (buymeonce.com).

Go paperless by opting for email correspondence

my musing

We are big fans of old school books and paper certainly still has its place, but excess paperwork is the worst. Opt for a clutter-free alternative and get into the habit of filing your emails.

resource: check it out

Try to be conscious and ask yourself questions around what you really need to print out or what can be done digitally/online.

Invest in a *pressure cooker*

my musing
A great investment for tasty meals while conserving energy at the same time. A pressure cooker allows you to create slow-cooked meals in half the time.

resource: invest
Try Breville's Fast Slow Pro cooker (breville.com).

ditch the tumble dryer

my musing
I'd choose sun-dried clothes as an alternative every time – you can't beat that fresh-off-the-line smell.

resource: **try this**
Opt for the Artiss Bamboo Clothes Drying Rack, which is all about eco-friendly drying.

· ·

Use a dishwasher

· ·

my musing
Any excuse for not doing the dishes!

resource: download
Canstar Blue's dishwasher review compares and
rates dishwashers on everything from performance
to value for money (canstarblue.com.au).

REUSE AND RECYCLE WATER

my musing

Something we should all get into the practice of doing.

resource: **buy**

The Yeti Loadout Bucket is strong and large, so you don't have to make as many trips lugging bathwater to your backyard (au.yeti.com).

"If it can't be reduced, reused, repaired, rebuilt, refurbished, refinished, resold, recycled, or composted, then it should be restricted, designed or removed from production."

– Jonathan Safran Foer

june shopping

As Vivienne Westwood famously said, 'Buy less, choose well.' I love this quote and wholeheartedly agree! I always try to research where my clothes or products come from, and try to be responsible in supporting brands that are ethical, sustainable and considered. I also try to keep an eye out for brand certificates so I can be sure a product has been made in socially and environmentally responsible conditions. This month let's delve into everything 'shopping', from ethics to fabrics to buying second-hand. There are lots of tips here to help you search for brands and products that have a mindful approach to our environment and their workers!

GET TO KNOW
WHERE TO BUY
ETHICAL CLOTHES

my musing
Find ethical brands that you love, and make them your go-to when it comes to buying new clothes.

resource: follow the link!

https://fairwear.org

Shop online

my musing

It's believed that 22 per cent of a garment's climate impact comes from the process of a consumer driving to a store to buy something. With so many great websites out there, make friends with online shopping.

resource: take a look

Eluxemagazine.com has a comprehensive list of sustainable fashion brands available to buy online.

Look for a brand's certifications

my musing

This is a great way to establish whether the product you're buying has been made in socially and environmentally responsible conditions.

resource: check online

Go to https://www.greenmatters.com/p/sustainable/ clothing/certifications for more information.

Avoid buying polyester and all synthetic fibres

my musing

Natural fibres are better for your skin, and better for the environment (if they're produced ethically and sustainably) - it's a win-win situation.

resource: learn

Trustedclothes.com is an informative resource for tips on avoiding synthetic fibres.

When buying activewear, look for polyester that's made from recycled water bottles, fishing nets, carpet, and other post-consumer products

my musing

Yes to this – I live in activewear most of the time and love how many labels are getting creative when it comes to their sustainability.

resource: read

Urban Sweat has a great article on five ethical, Aussie, activewear brands (urbansweat.com.au).

BUY BRANDS THAT PAY THEIR WORKERS FAIRLY

my musing

This is so important. Educate yourself when it comes to which brands you spend with, and don't buy into fast fashion.

resource: download

The Good On You app tells you how ethical fashion brands really are.

Shop
second-
hand

my musing

Whether a garage sale or a rummage around an op-shop, buying second-hand can unearth some stunning hidden gems.

resource: follow the link!

https://www.marieclaire.com.au/second-hand-clothes

Rent clothes for *special occasions*

my musing

I love this idea. If you've got a one-off event that you want to look a million dollars for, rather than buying something you'll never wear again, hire an outfit instead.

resource: **download the app**

The Outdress app connects renters with lenders in their local community to hire luxury brands, designer dresses, suits – you name it.

GO WITHOUT AND BUY LESS STUFF

my musing

Try the 24-hour rule before buying something. Often, if you take a step back, you'll realise that you don't really need what you thought you did.

resource: read

Read *The Year of Less* by blogger Cait Flanders.

CONTACT YOUR FAVOURITE BRANDS

my musing

Speak up if the brand you love isn't aligned with your ethics – a crucial way to create change for the better is to let our voices be heard.

resource: encourage

A simple search on the brand's website should give you the contact details you need to send them an email encouraging them to adopt a more sustainable practice.

Borrow books from libraries instead of buying online

my musing
Go old-school with your lending habits. And there are so many street libraries popping up now, too.

resource: search
Find what you want in a library near you with WorldCat, a global catalogue of library collections.

GET A DIGITAL SUBSCRIPTION

my musing

This is a great way to read your favourite magazine or newspaper and support journalists without producing unnecessary waste.

resource: **follow the link!**

https://www.isubscribe.com.au/digital.cfm

attend clothes swapping events

my musing

This is such a great idea and can be a fun way to spend the afternoon with friends. As the saying goes, one person's trash is another person's treasure.

resource: check it out

Go to events.clothingexchange.com.au to find an event near you.

Riffle
through a
flea market

my musing

Some of my best buys have been from flea markets
– and you just never know what you'll come across at
your local one!

resource: go online

Elle.com.au has a list of the best vintage flea markets
in Australia.

UNDERSTAND THAT NATURAL DOESN'T ALWAYS MEAN SUSTAINABLE

my musing
Get to know the difference, and shop according to your personal ethics.

resource: look it up
Look up treehugger.com for more information on the difference between natural and sustainable.

CREATE A CAPSULE *(AND ETHICAL)* WARDROBE

my musing

A capsule wardrobe (a small collection of versatile pieces that you can mix and match to create outfits for the season) is a great way to declutter and simplify things – after all, the less choice you have the easier deciding what to wear will be.

resource: follow the link!

https://www.marieclaire.com.au/ethical-capsule-wardrobe

Restyle instead of replacing old clothes

my musing

Think of alternative ways to transform your old clothes, such as dyeing or bleaching them, or wearing them in a completely different way.

resource: watch

There are lots of great tutorials on how to transform old clothing on YouTube. Jump on and be inspired.

Look after your clothes properly

♥

my musing

I'm all about this. Treat your clothes with respect and they'll last so much longer.

resource: search

Goodonyou.eco has an ultimate guide to making your clothes last that's well worth a read.

Invest in an *umbrella* with a *lifetime* guarantee

my musing

Because buying cheap umbrellas that don't last is a far more costly habit than a one-off investment.

resource: invest

The Davek 'Savile' umbrella is built to last (au.davekny.com).

Buy durable cookware

my musing

Stay away from cheap sets of cookware that will need to be replaced sooner – you might even find that you become a better cook as a result of it!

resource: buy things that last

Corningware sell a stunning French White bakeware set that's made to last for generations (shopcorellebrands.com.au).

CHOOSE AN ECO-FRIENDLY YOGA MAT

my musing

And with so many stunning mats on the market, you really are spoilt for choice. Look for sustainable rubber or cork mats.

resource: **namaste**

I love Manduka's range of mats (manduka.com).

Watch this space! Collective Hub has something coming soon!

Invest in decent pens that will last

my musing

Gone are the days of dozens of dried-up biros. One good pen is all you'll ever need.

resource: **reuse**

Biome's Baoer 3035 Stainless Steel Fountain Pen with a refillable ink cartridge is a great option for reducing excess waste (biome.com.au).

Question *yourself* before adding to your *wardrobe*

my musing

Do you really need it? Will it improve your life in any way? Are you impulse buying because you're bored or tired or unfulfilled? Get comfortable in questioning yourself before making any purchases and it will soon become a natural habit.

resource: read

Check out the article on Buymeonce.com for the five questions to ask yourself before buying new clothes.

SUPPORT RETAILERS DESIGNING PRODUCTS TO LAST

my musing

Yes to this – and there are lots of them out there if you look hard enough. Help make wasteful practices a thing of the past.

resource: buy longer-lasting items

Buymeonce.com only stocks products that they have found to be the longest-lasting version.

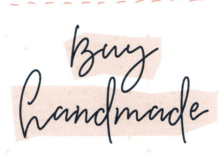

my musing

I love handmade pieces; I love their flaws and imperfections, and knowing that they've been made with warmth.

resource: jump online

Check out loveaustralianhandmade.com. Also take a look on our good friends Instagram @peacharoo.

Practice *mindfulness* when shopping

my musing
Being mindful and conscious of how we shop is a crucial way to change our shopping habits for the better.

resource: follow the link

https://thecalmcollective.com/mindful-shopping

- -

BUY YOUR BREAKFAST AND COFFEE ORDER FROM A SUSTAINABLE CAFE

- -

my musing

Remember, it's up to us as consumers to let our money do the talking.

resource: **drink to that**

The Urban List often lists the best sustainable cafes and restaurants in your city (theurbanlist.com).

Download an ethical shopping app

my musing

And you'll have everything you need to know about ethical shopping at the touch of a button.

resource: **check it out**

Try the Shop Ethical! app.

Learn how to mend your clothes

my musing
Go old-school when it comes to making the most out of your clothes.

resource: watch
Head to YouTube for some easy-to-follow videos on all things sewing.

BUY SUSTAINABLE STATIONERY

my musing

Because when you can have stylish and sustainable, the answer is always yes.

resource: jump online

Buyecogreen.com.au.

"Cheap fashion is really far from that, it may be cheap in terms of the financial cost, but very expensive when it comes to the environment and the cost of human life."

– Sass Brown

july
random acts
of kindness

I pondered over whether to include a chapter on random acts of kindness – after all, it's not the most obvious topic for a book on living ethically. But I'm a big believer in the power of warmth, generosity and compassion, and subsequently, kindness and living ethically are somewhat intertwined, for me at least. Few things warm my heart in the way that those good news stories do, and so I want to encourage you all to take a moment to think what you might be able to do today, tomorrow or this year to better the life of someone else, without expecting anything in return.

GIVE A STRANGER A COMPLIMENT

my musing

It's something I try to do as often as I can. A sincere and genuine compliment really can make someone's day.

resource: read

The Huffington Post has a wonderful article on the incredible power of a compliment (huffingtonpost.com.au).

Let someone go in front of you at the supermarket

my musing

If time is on your side and you can sense the person behind you is rushing – or even if they aren't – it's a small, but effective, good deed.

resource: suggestion

The Kind Blog has a whole host of other suggestions like this: https://www.randomactsofkindness.org/the-kindness-blog

Volunteer at a *charity shop*

my musing

There are a wealth of charity shops these days, so pick one with a cause close to your heart, and donate whatever time you might be able to.

resource: **find a local shop**

Have a look online for your nearest op-shop.

PICK UP LITTER

my musing
Yes to this one. Get into the habit of picking up litter when you see it, and soon you'll do it automatically.

resource: **suggestion**
Grab a litter picker from Amazon to make the job a little easier.

Visit someone in an old people's home

my musing

One day we might be that person in an aged care facility in want of a friendly face and some company. Take it upon yourself to brighten someone's day by offering to lend an ear – you might be surprised to find out you get just as much joy out of your visit as they do.

resource: listen

Agedcareguide.com.au has a complete list of nursing homes in your state.

Ask for charity donations *instead* of gifts

my musing

Because when it comes to birthday presents, most of us don't need any more than we already have. Choose a charity whose cause you believe in, and direct friends and family to donate to them instead.

resource: request a donation

Lifehack.org has a list of the charities where your money is actually going to help the people you want it to help.

HOLD OPEN DOORS FOR PEOPLE

my musing

Kind gestures like holding a door open can put a smile on even the sourest of faces. Take time to think about the little things that will brighten someone's day.

resource: listen

Christiaan Triebert has done a wonderful TED talk on 'The Beauty of Random Acts of Kindness'.

WALK AN ELDERLY NEIGHBOUR'S DOG

my musing

If you have an elderly or less-mobile neighbour, offering to walk their furry friend might be more helpful to them than you know.

resource: suggestion

"Do what you can, with what you have, where you are." – Theodore Roosevelt

Offer to babysit for a friend for free

my musing

If you've got friends who have a new baby or an unruly toddler, giving them the gift of time to themselves really is priceless.

resource: **quote of the day**

"No one has ever become poor by giving."
– Anne Frank

Do a favour for someone without expecting anything in return

my musing

Giving without expectations will help to further a movement of making the world a happier place.

resource: get inspired

Check out the Pay It Forward Foundation for more inspiration (payitforwardfoundation.org).

PEN A HANDWRITTEN LETTER TO A LOVED ONE

my musing

Do it to cultivate a little romance, nurture a friendship or simply stay connected with loved ones while abroad.

resource: **pen to paper!**

I love Papier's stationery for sending cards and notes (papier.com).

Spend the day at a soup kitchen

my musing

Because we could all do with recognising our own privilege and lending our time to those less fortunate than ourselves.

resource: give your time

Vinnies (vinnies.org.au), Foodbank Australia (foodbank.org.au) and Oz Harvest (ozharvest.org) can all point you in the right direction.

BUY A COFFEE FOR A PERSON IN THE LINE BEHIND YOU

my musing

I love this. A thoughtful deed that might just make someone's day.

resource: read

Headspace.com has a great blog called 'Why you should buy a coffee for the customer behind you.'

GIVE UP YOUR SEAT ON THE BUS FOR SOMEONE ELSE

my musing

Do it just because you can. You never know what someone else might be feeling - they might be living with invisible chronic pain or they might have had a bad day at work. A small gesture like this can make someone's day!

resource: listen

Try The Kindness Podcast with Nicole Phillips.

· ·

Say Thank you to a cleaner

· ·

my musing
Because having an attitude of gratitude is one of the best things you can do for your own well-being.

resource: tune in
Watch the short film *Gratitude* by Louie Schwartzberg.

Reconnect with an old friend

my musing
With the busyness of life, some friendships get overlooked. Reach out to someone you miss, because today is as good a day as any.

resource: reconnect
Forbes online have a great feature called 'The Power and Joy of Reconnecting with Old Friends' (forbes.com).

LEND YOUR SKILLS TO A START-UP

my musing

We've all got skills that someone out there could benefit from, and finding a start-up in need of some help, or a recent graduate who could do with some mentoring, will be a hugely rewarding endeavor.

resource: share your skills

Hunterfuturepreneurs.com.au can help match mentors with start-ups.

Support your friends' Businesses

my musing

This is crucial. A Facebook like, a social share, a shoutout on Instagram... none of them cost you a penny, yet they really can make the world of difference to a business.

resource: jump online

Bossbabe.com has a great blog on ways in which you can support your friends' businesses.

CHEER MARATHON RUNNERS ON

my musing

This is one of the best ways to reinstall your faith in humanity. There is so much joy to be had from watching the collective coming together of people at a marathon. And the runners gain so much strength from this one small act.

resource: read

Read The Washington Post's article 'If you are losing faith in human nature, go out and watch a marathon' (washingtonpost.com).

TELL YOUR FAMILY THAT YOU LOVE THEM

my musing

Life is short, and often fragile. Tell someone special that you love them, just because.

resource: quote

"Never stop showing someone how much they mean to you." - Unknown

Visit someone in hospital

my musing

It's easy to see hospital visits as a hassle, but an hour or two of your time can mean so, so much to those in need.

resource: plug in

Lovlist.org have a guide on dealing with a loved one in hospital.

Stop and *speak* to a homeless *person*

my musing

Let them know that you see them, and you hear them. Taking away their invisibility for a minute might be the best thing that happens to them that day.

resource: **tune in**

Watch 'Can a Haircut change Your Life: The Story of Us' with Joshua Coombes.

Make a loved one Breakfast in Bed

my musing

Set your alarm for half an hour earlier, then get up and whip up some smashed avo or scrambled eggs for your significant other.

resource: try something new

BBC Good Food has an excellent collection of impressive breakfast-in-bed recipes (bbcgoodfood.com).

ARRANGE A DIRECT DEBIT TO A CHARITY CLOSE TO YOUR HEART

my musing

A monthly donation to a charity can truly make a difference to people most in need of our help.

resource: give back

Changepath.com.au has a helpful guide on the best Australian charities.

Set an intention for someone you love

my musing

Instead of setting an intention for yourself, do it for a friend or a family member. It can be a really powerful way of communicating your love for them.

resource: jump online

Sarahprout.com has some practical advice for intention-setting.

Bring *treats* to work for your *coworkers*

my musing

Help your team get through an afternoon slump and bring a little treat to work! Because everyone loves an afternoon sugar hit.

resource: **get inspired**

Buy *Party Food to Share* by Kathy Kordalis.

Pay extra at the parking meter

my musing

Next time you park in a metered spot, pay for an hour longer than you need so the next person to park there gets a nice surprise

resource: read

Read *The Little Book of Kindness* by Bernadette Russell.

OFFER A HOMELESS PERSON YOUR LEFTOVERS BAG FROM THE RESTAURANT, OR BUY THEM A TAKEAWAY

my musing

Not only are you stopping someone from going hungry, you're also doing your bit for the planet by reducing food waste.

resource: make a difference

Metro.co.uk has a wonderful article called 'These formerly homeless people have shared the best things you can do to really make a difference'

LET SOMEONE INTO YOUR LANE. THEY'RE PROBABLY IN A RUSH, JUST LIKE YOU

my musing
Nobody needs road rage in their lives. And you'll learn not to rush through life in the process.

resource: tune in
Listen to the Rich Thoughts for Happy Lives podcast by Coady Bennett.

august

self-love

Self-love comes in many shapes and sizes. It can be cultivating compassion; it can come in the form of spending time in nature; and sometimes it can simply be giving yourself permission to say no to something that you feel obliged to say yes to. Whatever self-love looks like to you, I hope these suggestions inspire and encourage you to take some time out for you, this month, and always.

FORGIVE SOMEONE WHO HAS HURT YOU IN THE PAST

my musing

Forgiveness is one of the most powerful things you can do. Forgive often.

resource: watch

Head to The Mindful Movement's YouTube channel for a forgiveness meditation.

Start the morning with a sunrise

my musing

My favourite way to start the day. Put yourself in the way of beauty as frequently as you can.

resource: **read**

Lonelyplanet.com has a great article on where to see the world's best sunrises

SPEND TIME IN NATURE

my musing

Yes to this! Get out in the open, swim in the sea, go on a hike, and walk barefoot in the sand. Connecting with nature is one of the best things you can do for both your mind and your body.

resource: read

Tourism Australia is a great resource for the country's best coastal walks (australia.com).

Meditate

my musing

Get into the practice of doing it daily. Think you're too busy to meditate? As the proverb goes: 'If you don't have time to meditate for 5 minutes, then meditate for an hour'.

resource: **get the apps!**

Calm and Headspace are my go-to apps for all things meditation.

ALLOW YOURSELF AN HOUR, DAY OR WEEK OF REST

my musing

Stop glorifying being busy and carve out some time in your weekly schedule where you allow yourself to do absolutely nothing – without feeling guilty about it.

resource: delve in

Read *The Book Of Rest: Stop Striving, Start Being* by Gabrielle Brown.

Treat *yourself* to a massage

my musing

The ultimate treat to yourself. You'll be amazed at what a massage can do for your well-being.

resource: **research**

Virgin Australia has a great write-up on 'The 6 Most Indulgent Spa Retreats in Australia'.

Go wild swimming

my musing

Come rain or shine, a bit of salt or fresh water therapy is one of the most invigorating and rejuvenating things you can do for yourself.

resource: feel free

Read *Wild Swimming: Sydney, Australia* by Sally Tertini. And check out wildswimmingaustralia.com to discover wild swimming holes across Australia.

**ask
for help**

my musing
Allowing yourself to be vulnerable isn't easy for a lot of us, but as the great professor and author Brené Brown said: 'Vulnerability is not weakness; it's our greatest measure of courage.'

resource: watch
Watch Michele L Sullivan's TED talk, 'Asking for help is a strength, not a weakness.'

GO PHONE-FREE FOR AN EXTENDED PERIOD OF TIME

my musing

I'm all about the digital detox. So many of us spend our days glued to our mobiles, it's almost impossible to remember what life was like without them. Taking regular breaks from technology will help you live more in the present, reduce stress and increase happiness.

resource: be aware

Read *How to Break Up with Your Phone* by Catherine Price.

Declutter your apartment

my musing

I moved house recently into a much smaller unit, which meant a *lot* of decluttering. Getting rid of things that you no longer need is good for the soul.

resource: declutter

Read *The Life-Changing Magic of Tidying Up* by Marie Kondo.

MAKE A VISION BOARD

my musing
Because a dream becomes a goal when action is taken towards achieving it.

resource: search online
A quick YouTube search on vision boards will give you some practical guidance, or jump onto my Instagram @lisamessenger circa July 2020 and you'll see a full video on creating a huge vision wall that we created in my home office.

TAKE SOME TIME OUT OF YOUR DAY FOR SOME BREATH WORK

my musing

Create some time in your day to embrace stillness and concentrate on your breathing – the wealth of benefits is endless.

resource: **download**

Download the Reach Out Breathe app to help you relax and focus on your breathing.

spend some time journaling

my musing

I love journaling at both the beginning and end of the day – it's a great way to evoke mindfulness and can help us regulate our emotions.

resource: check out our journals!

My team and I have designed some incredible journaling products for you! Check them out at collectivehub.com

Write a list of *everything* you're grateful for

my musing

Because gratitude really is everything. When I write my gratitudes every morning it really helps set the intention for my day ahead in the best way possible.

resource: **write!**

Buy yourself a notebook or journal and make listing out your gratitudes a priority before delving into your working day. Try Collective Hub's *Daily Gratitudes Journal* for (we think) the best gratitudes journal you'll get your hands on. Collectivehub.com.

Swap screen time for face time

my musing

Get off your phone and arrange to see a loved one face-to-face, rather than communicating via Instagram or WhatsApp.

resource: go without

Elitedaily.com has a fab article on 10 easy ways to use your phone less.

MOVE!

my musing

I love a morning dance – it's how I start most days. I've also recently invested in a treadmill which I jump on often for a quick sweat sesh! However, if you like to move, make it a non-negotiable.

resource: be accountable for yourself

Download the Activity Tracker app to your phone and pay attention to how much you do or don't move each day.

Walk barefoot in the sand

my musing
And revel in the beauty of Mother Nature.

resource: read
Vogue.com.au's article 'Australia's 50 most beautiful beaches' will give you some sandy inspiration.

Learn a new skill

my musing
Because staying curious is one of the best things you can do.

resource: **learn**
Check out udemy.com for everything from creativity workshops with Elizabeth Gilbert to yoga teacher training.

SAY NO

my musing

If it's not a hell yes, it's a no.

resource: read

Read *F**k No!: How to Stop Saying Yes When You Can't, You Shouldn't, or You Just Don't Want To* by Sarah Knight.

SAY
YES

my musing

Be open to every opportunity that comes your way. Step out of your comfort zone – you might be surprised by what you find there.

resource: delve in

Read *The Year of Yes: How to Dance It Out, Stand in the Sun and Be Your Own Person* by Shonda Rhimes.

Go on a date with your city

my musing
Because it's one of the best kind of dates you can go on. Explore what your local surrounds have to offer!

resource: explore
Nationalgeographic.com's guide on how to be a tourist in your own home town is well worth a read.

Visit somewhere you've *always* wanted to go

my musing

Go exploring. Dream bigger and discover things you've always wanted to discover. You won't regret it!

resource: jump online

Travelocity.com have compiled a list of 10 cities that should be on everyone's bucket list.

PRACTICE COMPASSION

my musing

Because everyone is fighting a battle you know nothing about. Be kind, always.

resource: tune in

Listen to the Being Well Podcast on Growing Compassion & Kindness with Dr Rick Hanson.

WRITE YOURSELF A LOVE LETTER

my musing

Since it's so easy to talk about what you don't like about yourself, why not go out of your comfort zone and write down some of the things that you actually do?

resource: journal

Get yourself a copy of our *Create Your Best Life Journal* from collectivehub.com for a whole lot of self love guideance!

Write a letter of encouragement to your future self

my musing

Picturing yourself a year from now and outlining what you want to achieve might just be the best way to make it a reality.

resource: get inspired

Check out Futureme.org for some letter inspiration.

CREATE A BEAUTIFUL SANCTUARY IN YOUR BEDROOM

my musing
Because home really is where the heart is.

resource: style
Have a look at Crystalbaileyandco.com for some seriously stylish interior inspo.

READ

my musing
The benefits are boundless. From being more educated, to expanding your vocabulary, feeling more relaxed and taking time out!

resource: invest
Thelitedit.com has reading recommendations and literary tidbits aplenty.

Spend longer in bed

my musing

Do it just because you can!

resource: watch

Read *Why We Sleep: The New Science of Sleep and Dreams* by Matthew Walker.

INVEST IN A SESSION WITH A REIKI MASTER, KINESIOLOGIST OR THERAPIST

my musing

Alternative therapies can be one of the most healing endeavours for your mind, body and spirit.

resource: try it out!

Consciouspanda.com have a write-up on the reasons why you need reiki in your life.

Make a *nourishing* meal

my musing
And eat yourself happy.

resource: purchase
Buy *The Nourishing Cook* by Leah Itsines.

Banish negative thoughts

my musing
Master your mindset and revel in the power of positive thinking.

resource: tune in
Have a listen to the Live Happy Now podcast (livehappy.com).

september travel

Travel, for many people (myself included), is an integral part of life. Whether you travel for business, for pleasure, or both, it is your right and your choice to do so. I certainly know my life would be a lot less rich were it not for the people I meet and the places I see when I travel. That being said, there is no denying the effect travel can have on the environment, and I am certainly looking at ways in which I can reduce my carbon footprint and become a more conscious, intentional traveller. From calculating your carbon footprint to embracing the art of slow travel, I hope some of these suggestions will aid you in your adventures – whether overseas or in your own backyard. Need some more tips and planning advice on your next adventure? Get your hands on our *Ultimate Travel Journal* available at collectivehub.com.

CHOOSE AN AIRLINE WITH A CARBON OFFSET PROGRAM

my musing

This is becoming more and more common among airlines, so be sure that when you fly, you do so as sustainably as you can.

resource: get inspired

A quick search online will give you an idea of which airlines have carbon offset programs.

When going overseas, opt for fewer, longer flights

my musing

The biggest impact on the environment comes from the take-off and landing when flying, so choose longer flights if you can, and take pleasure in some technology-free travel time.

resource: compare

Use flight comparison sites such as Skyscanner.com to ensure you're taking as few flights as possible

Calculate your *carbon footprint* and donate accordingly

my musing

This is such a great idea. If, like me, you want to become a more mindful traveller, this carbon calculator calculates your footprint and suggests where, and how much, you should donate to offset it.

resource: **check out**

Carbonfootprint.com has a great calculator you can use.

EXPLORE YOUR OWN CITY

my musing

It's so easy to become complacent about the city in which we live. Instead of planning an overseas adventure, book yourself into a hotel or Airbnb in a neighbourhood you don't know, and play tourist for the weekend.

resource: staycation

Sitchu.com.au has a wonderful selection of online neighbourhood guides.

Travel by road or rail

my musing

Flying might be quicker, but there's no doubt it's much worse for the environment – so why not enjoy a long, relaxing train journey instead, with a great book to keep you company?

resource: read

Nationalrail.com has a write-up on four reasons taking the train is better for the environment that's worth a read.

Walk, cycle or take public transport when travelling

my musing

With taxis just a click away, it's easy to rely on them when getting around a new city. But one of the best ways to get to know somewhere new is on foot, on a bike, or by using the local public transport.

resource: read

Check out Lonelyplanet.com's article on how to go green when you travel.

EMBRACE
THE ART OF
SLOW TRAVEL

my musing

Slow travel is a mindset that rejects traditional ideas of tourism and encourages you to soak in your environments and keep yourself open to new experiences. Make this year a time to be intentional when you travel.

resource: check out

Read *The Idle Traveller: The Art of Slow Travel* by Dan Kieran.

CHOOSE AN ETHICAL TRAVEL DESTINATION

my musing

With ethical travel destinations including the likes of Fiji and Nepal, there's never been a better time to travel ethically. Ethical travel means you are benefitting the people and environment where you're spending time (and money).

resource: listen

Listen to The Ethical Traveler Podcast for ideas.

Stay in eco accommodation

my musing

With a wealth of eco options now available – from glamping to elegant lodges – gone are the days when eco accommodation meant compromising on your creature comforts.

resource: follow the link

Ecobnb.com and greengetaways.com.au

Choose a local tour guide or travel company

my musing

Always go local when it comes to tour guides; you'll not only be supporting the country you're visiting, but more often than not you'll also get a more authentic cultural experience.

resource: go local

Viator is the industry leader in tours, activities, attraction tickets and local tour guides, with more than 1300 destinations worldwide (viator.com).

Avoid animal tourism at all costs

my musing

You may want to get up close and personal with a country's wild animals, but animal tourism is rarely, if ever, ethical.

resource: download

Intrepidtravel.com have an easy-to-follow online guide for ethical animal tourism.

Know when, and when not, to volunteer

my musing

It's tempting to think that volunteering abroad is a selfless act and a good way to give back to the country you're visiting– but it's essential that you do your research before you volunteer.

resource: do your research

Nomadic Matt has written a well-researched blog on how to volunteer abroad (nomadicmatt.com).

PACK RESPONSIBLY

my musing

Travel-sized beauty products may seem like a great way of minimising your luggage load, but in reality they often cause excess and unnecessary waste. Paying attention to the amount of waste you produce – especially when travelling – is an integral part of sustainable travel.

resource: try

Try eco-friendly products such as Ethique Solid Shampoo, Raw Elements sunscreen and Coconut Matter Mood Deodorant. If you must carry travel-sized containers, opt for plastic-free reusable sets, such as Biome's Plastic Free Zero Waste Travel Container Kit (biome.com.au).

Leave
a light
footprint

my musing
Whatever that looks like to you, do what you can to travel as lightly as possible.

resource: read
1millionwomen.org have a fantastic article on how to leave nothing but footprints.

DONATE

my musing

Find a charity that does important work in the country or city you're visiting, and if you're able to do so, consider making a small donation at the end of your trip.

resource: learn

Intentionaltravelers.com offers handy advice on how best to donate when you travel.

EAT LOCALLY SOURCED FOOD

my musing

One of the best ways to get a true experience of a place that you're visiting is by eating locally. Avoid chain restaurants, step out of your comfort zone and try a local delicacy. Your taste buds will thank you for it.

resource: tune in!

Listen to the Look Like a Local: Travelers Not Tourists podcast by Joel Hiscutt.

Celebrate and support local culture

my musing

Whether that means attending a local festival or visiting an indigenous museum, look beyond the well-trodden tourist path to fully embrace the culture of the country you're visiting.

resource: **head to**

http://www.nomadicdreamer.com/5-ways-to-travel-sustainably-support-local-cultures/

my musing

With ongoing commitments to make the world a more
environmentally friendly place, put cities such as
Portland and Amsterdam on your must-visit travel list.

resource: take a look online

Lonelyplanet.com has an excellent selection of
articles on green cities.

Take a staycation

my musing
Because sometimes the best adventures to be had are on your own doorstep.

resource: **read**
This Is Where You Belong: Finding Home Wherever You Are by Melody Warnick.

Spend your money locally

my musing

Well-known shops and restaurants can be a safe bet when stocking up on supplies and eating out when abroad – but next time you travel, commit to spending your money at local stores and eateries.

resource: follow the link

http://blog.grassrootsvolunteering.org/how-to-spend-locally-while-traveling/

CONSIDER RENTING A HYBRID OR ELECTRIC VEHICLE

my musing

If you need to drive while you're away, a hybrid car is a fantastic option for a green way to get around.

resource: research

Hertz Green Collection offers hybrid cars for hire (hertz.com.au).

TAKE LEFTOVER SOAPS AND TOILETRIES WITH YOU TO AVOID UNNECESSARY WASTE

my musing

Hotel toiletries are an indulgent novelty when travelling, but they too are a culprit for unnecessary waste. If you do use yours, but don't finish them during your stay, take them with you to get maximum usage, and be sure to recycle them afterwards.

resource: jump online

Telegraph.co.uk has an interesting article on what happens to leftover hotel toiletries.

Stick to the path when hiking

my musing

Quite simply, it will help preserve trail systems for generations to come.

resource: read the tips

Check out NPS.gov's 'Hike Smart' tips.

DON'T BUY SOUVENIRS MADE FROM ENDANGERED PLANTS OR ANIMALS

my musing

And, unless there's a souvenir you particularly want, make do with memories instead – they're guaranteed to last a lifetime.

resource: follow the link

https://timetravelbee.com/bee-eco/responsible-shopping-guide/

Never feed or touch wildlife

my musing

More often than not, it does more harm than good. Admire them from a distance and leave them alone.

resource: plug in

PETA is an excellent resource for tips on how to behave around local wildlife (peta.org).

Be *respectful* of the local culture

my musing

Dress appropriately, act accordingly, and, if in doubt, ask. It's also a good idea to ask your travel agent about local cultures and appropriate etiquette.

resource: **go online**

https://www.kayak.com.au/news/travel-etiquette-tips/

Always choose economy class

my musing

Business or First Class may make for a more comfortable flight, as I travel so much for work on long haul flights, I am definitely guilty of opting for business class when I can – I am terrible without sleep, but such luxury comes at an environmental cost.

resource: peruse

Skyscanner.ae has 10 hacks to make your Economy flight feel like it's First Class.

AVOID THE
MINI BAR

my musing

Another novel part of hotel stays, but also an offender when it comes to excess waste. Avoid.

resource: follow the link

https://www.vogue.com/article/eco-friendly-hotels-that-are-serious-about-going-plastic-free

Leave the 'Do Not Disturb' sign on the door of your room for the duration of your stay.

my musing

Having freshly laundered sheets and a room that's cleaned daily is a luxury many of us love, but it also leaves a greater carbon footprint in its wake.

resource: jump online

https://www.nytimes.com/2018/02/27/travel/skipping-hotel-housekeeping-perks.html

Pack recyclable cutlery for your trip

my musing

If you'll be eating on-the-fly, cut down on your plastic consumption by packing some reusable cutlery.

resource: **buy**

Temple & Webster have a great stainless steel travel cutlery set for sale.

"Sustainability is *no longer* about doing *less harm.* It's about doing *more good.*"

– Jochen Zeitz

october
entertaining and christmas

If you're anything like me, you'll love a bit of entertaining. Whether it's a get-together with girlfriends, a casual Sunday brunch or a wholesome dinner for two, few things bring me greater joy in life than hosting loved ones for a few sacred hours of together-time. But, it has to be said, the entertainment market is saturated with disposable and throwaway paraphernalia that often goes straight to landfill the second the party is over. Here are some ideas on how to be the hostess with the mostest, without sacrificing on sustainability.

USE LOCAL FOLIAGE TO DECORATE

my musing
A really lovely way to add a special touch to the home; I love anything green, earth or nature-based when it comes to decorating.

resource: get into nature
I love Leaf Supply for anything plant related (leaf-supply.com).

Avoid balloons, streamers and anything that can't be reused or recycled

my musing

A good way to save your money and the planet at the same time.

resource: go minimal

Minimalist Living have a great video on YouTube on how to host a great dinner party.

USE PARAFFIN-FREE CANDLES ON THE TABLE

my musing

I love using candles to create a cosy and intimate feeling at home, but until I looked into it I didn't know that a lot of candles are made using paraffin, which is considered highly unsustainable. From now on I'll be opting for natural beeswax ones.

resource: check out

Try Happyflame.com.au for beeswax alternatives.

SERVE TAP WATER, SUSTAINABLE WINE AND FAIRTRADE COFFEE

my musing
Forget fancy cocktails and go green with your drinks next time you host friends.

resource: go green
Taylors Wines are a good place to start for sustainable options (taylorswines.com.au).

Send paperless invitations

my musing

Forget killing trees for the sake of an invitation and go online instead to send a vertual invitation. Or, if you do like the tradition of printed invitations, make sure you go for a sustainable paper option.

resource: try this!

Greenvelope.com is my go-to for this.

Donate unwanted food to a soup kitchen

my musing

If you're anything like me you'll over-prepare for guests when hosting, so if you have surplus food after a party, make sure it goes to people in need.

resource: **donate**

Oz Harvest can collect unwanted food and donate it to where it's needed.

IF USING CATERERS, MAKE SURE THEY'RE SUSTAINABLE

my musing

Be mindful of which caterers you use, and be sure to do your research before booking.

resource: try this!

A quick online search will help you find some local to your area. Try orderin.com.au for sustainable catering near you.

Rent tablecloths, napkins and dinnerware

my musing
Renting can be a cost effective and stylish alternative to throwaway party pieces that you'll use once in a blue moon.

resource: hire!
Simmonslinenhire.com.au has a gorgeous selection of linens available.

Choose gifts that last

my musing
Yes to this! Put some thought into gifts you give and choose presents that will stand the test of time.

resource: be thoughtful
Beautiful coffee table books are one of my favourite gifts to give.

GIFT A LOVED ONE WITH AN EXPERIENCE

my musing
As someone who collects memories, not things, I love the idea of being gifted with an experience.

resource: have some fun!
Try Redballoon.com.au for some inspiration.

Get creative with wrapping paper

my musing

Instead of buying an expensive roll of wrapping paper that will likely end up in the bin, try reusing newspaper for a vintage feel, or wrap gifts in a piece of fabric, tied in a knot.

resource: get some tips

Pinterest is a great resource for wrapping ideas using old newspaper. And have a look at https://www.1millionwomen.com.au/blog/how-furoshiki-japanese-fabric-wrapping/

Choose one big present

my musing

Forget a festive stocking full of novelty knick-knacks, and choose just one thoughtful, more personal gift.

resource: go big

Science Daily released an interesting study called 'The Paradox of gift giving,' which is well worth a read (sciencedaily.com).

GET CRAFTY WITH YOUR GIFTS AND MAKE YOUR OWN

my musing

If you're the creative type why not roll up your sleeves and make something yourself.

resource: check out

YouTube has some great videos on DIY gift making.

USE
HANDCRAFTED
DECORATIONS

my musing
Homemade decorations are a lovely way to add an intimate feel to any home at Christmas.

resource: read
Check *Gather at Home* by Monika Hibbs for ideas.

Switch to eco-friendly crackers (or don't use them at all)

my musing

If you can't do without crackers at Christmas, choose an eco brand for a greener Christmas Day – or why not make your own?

resource: purchase

Christmaselves.com.au has a lovely set of eco Christmas crackers.

REUSE DECORATIONS

my musing

Move away from the throwaway culture that has become so much a part of society, and get into the habit of storing decorations and reusing them each year – better for both your wallet and the planet.

resource: **repurpose**

Countryliving.com has some handy tips on how to repurpose Christmas decorations.

Rent a Christmas tree

my musing
Cost-effective and sustainable, what's not to love?

resource: pin!
Head to Thechristmastreecompany.com.au for
a beautiful range of trees.

Turn your houseplant into a festive focal point

my musing

I love dressing up a big house plant for a festive centrepiece, and it can be an elegant alternative to a Christmas tree, without the falling pine needles.

resource: get inspired

Head online for inspiration – Pinterest is your friend here (pinterest.com.au).

Send e-cards or make a charity donation instead

my musing

Time efficient, cost effective and oh-so-much better for the planet. Make the switch to e-cards this year if you haven't already.

resource: you've got mail

Hallmarkecards.com have an impressive selection – whatever your style and taste.

CUT FOOD WASTE BY USING ALL LEFTOVERS

my musing

From salads to risottos to pies, use your festive leftovers to do some tasty meal prep for the week ahead.

resource: jump online

Taste.com.au has a whole selection of recipes made from festive leftovers.

Use eco dinnerware

my musing

If it's time to invest in some new plates for the silly season, opt for an eco-brand if you're able to do so.

resource: check out

I love the brand Wasara (wasara.jp).

Ask for charity donations instead of gifts

my musing

I love this. Unless there's something you've been lusting over for ages, why not ask friends and family to donate to a charity on your behalf?

resource: give back

Create an online registry for donations at
Thegoodregistry.com

USE LED CHRISTMAS LIGHTS

my musing

Simply because they're more sustainable than the traditional alternative.

resource: jump online

Bunnings stocks LED lights that are both lovely and inexpensive.

Shop *locally* and *Fairtrade*

my musing

Avoid shopping centres like the plague near Christmas and opt instead for local boutiques and markets.

resource: be conscious

Fairtrade.com.au has a wonderful conscious Christmas gift guide.

Buy a homeless person Christmas dinner

my musing

And in doing so count your blessings for all that you have. If you have time, stop and have a chat, see how else you can help, and wish them a lovely Christmas.

resource: **care more**

Wayside Chapel (waysidechapel.org.au) and The Salvation Army (salvationarmy.org.au) are good starting points for this.

ENCOURAGE GUESTS TO CARPOOL

my musing

If you're hosting and have multiple family members visiting, encourage them all to share rides and, in turn, save the planet.

resource: share the trip

Check out carpoolclub.com.au for tips and tricks on carpooling.

Source *local* food

my musing

Head to nearby farmers' markets and local butchers and fishmongers for your festive fare.

resource: **markets!**

Check out Farmersmarkets.org.au to find your local farmers' market.

Use scented pine cones to decorate

my musing

A lovely way to add a festive touch to your home this Christmas. Think cinnamon and clove for a hit of nostalgia. They also make a nice touch when attached to gifts too.

resource: make your own

YouTube has some handy videos on DIY scented pine cones. If you can't forage for pine cones, you can usually find them in craft stores or online.

CREATE NATURE-INSPIRED TABLE SETTINGS

my musing

Perfect for anyone who likes a bit of boho-luxe around their home. I love earthy table settings all year round.

resource: read

Search Pinterest for some stunning table inspo. Think sprigs of rosemary tucked into ribbon-tied napkins, while eucalyptus or succulent wreaths can make beautiful table centrepieces.

make your own rustic wreath

my musing
Because they're almost always better than their shop-bought counterparts – and they're so much fun to make.

resource: read and watch!
Read *Wreaths: Fresh, Foraged & Dried Floral Arrangements* by Katie Smyth and Terri Chandler. There are also some lovely DIY twig wreath tutorials on YouTube.

"WE CAN SIT BACK, DO NOTHING AND WATCH OUR PLANET BE DESTROYED. OR WE CAN TAKE ACTION, BECOME ADVOCATES AND START MAKING LIFESTYLE CHOICES WHICH ARE KINDER TO PEOPLE AND THE PLANET."

– Kira Simpson

november

sustainable causes
to support

If you're in a financial position to do so, there are a great many sustainable causes that need your support. Whether you want to donate to a wildlife charity or a campaign that is dealing with climate change, here are some worthy movements to get behind.

SLOW FOOD

my musing

Slow Food is a global, grassroots organisation, founded in 1989 to prevent the disappearance of local food cultures and traditions, counteract the rise of fast life and combat people's dwindling interest in the food they eat, where it comes from and how our food choices affect the world around us.

resource: Slowfood.com

Charity Water

my musing

Charity Water is an NYC-based organisation working in 28 developing countries, bringing clean water to people in need.

resource: **check out**

Charitywater.org

International Campaign to Ban Landmines (ICBL)

my musing

ICBL, 1997 Nobel Peace Prize Co-Laureate, works with the Mine Ban Treaty for a world without landmines

resource: Icbl.org

my musing

Sierra Club focuses on moving beyond fossil fuel dependency and preserving wild spaces from harmful development, as well as offering signature wilderness trek experiences to individuals across the country.

resource:

Sierraclub.org

EARTH ISLAND INSTITUTE

my musing

Earth Island nourishes ambitious fledgling projects, giving them fuel to thrive and potentially become independent nonprofits, such as Rainforest Action Network and Salmon Protection and Watershed Network. The California-based organisation has several locally focused initiatives under its wing, as well as international projects like the Center for Safe Energy and the Plastic Pollution Coalition, among many others. Supporters can pick and choose which project they'd like to fund.

resource: Earthisland.org

OCEAN CONSERVANCY

my musing

Ocean Conservancy works to keep the ocean healthy, to keep us healthy. Current areas of focus include addressing ocean acidification, restoration and oil spill recovery in the Gulf of Mexico, and protecting the Arctic ecosystem from damage by increased shipping and oil and gas exploration.

resource: Oceanconservancy.org

Earth Justice

my musing

Earthjustice is an independent crusade focusing on high-impact, precedent-setting battles run by dedicated, experienced lawyers taking on the David and Goliath fights many of us feel powerless to influence.

resource:

Earthjustice.org

Rainforest Alliance

my musing

Rainforest Alliance has gained public recognition with their independent certification of common rainforest products, such as chocolate, coffee, bananas and tea. Producers must meet strict sustainability standards to gain certification. The Alliance also works with foresters and the tourism industry in ecologically vulnerable areas.

resource:

Rainforest-alliance.org

my musing
A 'bold and fearless voice for justice and the planet'. Recent campaigns have targeted bee-killing neonicotinoid pesticides, 'dirty' tar sands oil extraction, and the environmental devastation associated with palm oil production.

resource: Foei.org

GREENPEACE

my musing

Made famous in the 1970s and '80s for its seafaring bands of activists peacefully accosting whaling ships and exposing covert nuclear testing, today's Greenpeace describes climate change as 'the number one threat facing our planet'.

resource:

Greenpeace.org.au

Environmental Working Group (EWG)

my musing

Known for their annual 'Dirty Dozen' list revealing the highest (and lowest) pesticide concentrations in conventionally grown produce, EWG is recognised for researching and spreading awareness regarding toxic chemicals, sustainable versus exploitative agricultural practices, consumer product safety, and corporate accountability.

resource: Ewg.org

NATURAL RESOURCES DEFENSE COUNCIL (NRDC)

my musing

Called 'One of the nation's most powerful environmental groups' by the New York Times, NRDC combines 'the grassroots power of 1.4 million members and online activists with the courtroom clout and expertise of more than 350 lawyers, scientists and other professionals.'

resource:

Nrdc.org

Union of Concerned Scientists (UCS)

my musing

UCS maintains a national network of nearly 17,000 scientists who believe 'rigorous analysis is the best way to understand the world's pressing problems and develop effective solutions to them.' UCS's findings and statements are frequently quoted by major news sources; they have become a recognised and respected voice of environmental advocacy. Their work focuses on clean energy solutions, global warming and the puzzles around large-scale food production. UCS's testimony has been instrumental in several pieces of important green legislation.

resource: Ucsusa.org

Defenders of Wildlife

my musing

The mission of Defenders of Wildlife is to protect and restore endangered wildlife across North America and beyond. Over the years, Defenders of Wildlife has fought for the conservation of green sea turtles, red wolves, Florida manatees and the prairie chicken, and constantly fights for the preservation of wildlife habitats.

resource:

Defenders.org

GLOBAL FOOTPRINT NETWORK

my musing

Founded in 2003, Global Footprint Network has obtained an impressive number of international awards for its work. The organisation's mission is to help companies, governments and individuals make wiser, more sustainable ecological decisions by offering actionable insights into natural resource management, resource consumption and capacity.

resource: Footprintnetwork.org

INTERNATIONAL FUND FOR ANIMAL WELFARE (IFAW)

my musing

The mission of the International Fund for Animal Welfare is to protect the natural habitats of animals and prevent their extinction. IFAW has offices in 15 countries and engages in wildlife protection programs in 40 countries.

resource:

lfaw.org

Earth Day Network

my musing

Earth Day Network are the main organisation behind Earth Day, but apart from this initiative they also engage in many other projects that raise awareness on climate change, fight deforestation and poverty, restore the urban tree canopy and mobilise the population through environmental and climate literacy.

resource: Earthday.org

Marine Conservation Institute

my musing

The Marine Conservation Institute's main project is the Global Ocean Refuge System, a science-based, collaborative and international effort designed to catalyse strong protection for at least 30% of the world's oceans by 2030.

resource:

Marine-conservation.org

WILDLIFE DIRECT

my musing

Wildlife Direct has offices in Kenya and the US, and empowers communities to peacefully coexist with wildlife. Some of their most notable programs include Fashion4Wildlife, Education and Outreach and NTV Wild.

resource: Wildlifedirect.org

NATIONAL AUDUBON SOCIETY

my musing

Through state programs, nature centres, chapters and partners, the National Audubon Society protects birds and the places where they live.

resource:

Audubon.org

Population Matters

my musing

Their vision is of a sustainable future, with decent living standards, environmental sustainability and a stable population size within resource constraints.

resource: Populationmatters.org

Go Green Week

my musing

Britain's largest student network campaigning about world poverty, human rights and the environment. Go Green Week is People & Planet's annual national week of climate action in schools, colleges and universities.

resource:

Peopleandplanet.org

The Climate Reality Project

my musing

Founded by former US Vice President Al Gore, The Climate Reality Project is bringing the world together to cut carbon pollution and create a healthy and prosperous future powered by clean energy.

resource: Climaterealityproject.org

Planting Peace

my musing

Planting Peace has purchased 624 acres of Peruvian rainforest land, which has now been placed in a land trust and is 100 per cent shielded from destruction. The hope is to continue to buy land around the existing reserve so it can expand its parameters, thus expanding the protective practices of the Amazon.

resource:

Plantingpeace.org

ONE WORLD ONE OCEAN

my musing

One World One Ocean is a media campaign by Oscar-nominated MacGillivray Freeman Films that uses film, TV and digital to promote protection of the oceans.

resource:

Oneworldoneocean.com

december
Global charities that need relief

It is impossible not to feel helpless at times. I know I have spent much of the beginning of 2020 watching in horror as the country I live in and love has gone up in flames. What it has taught me is this: the world needs our help, and the future is very much in our hands if we choose to take responsibility, action and accountability. There are many notable charities all over the world doing great things to better the lives of the planet, the people and the animals we know and love. Here's just a small selection of global charities in need of relief. If you are in a position to donate, know that every cent counts, however small it might seem to you.

PETA

my musing

People for the Ethical Treatment of Animals (PETA) is the largest animal rights organisation in the world, with more than 6.5 million members and supporters. PETA focuses its attention on the four areas in which the largest numbers of animals suffer the most intensely for the longest periods of time: in laboratories, in the food industry, in the clothing trade and in the entertainment industry. They also work on a variety of other issues, including the cruel killing of rodents, birds and other animals who are often considered 'pests', as well as cruelty to domesticated animals.

website: Peta.org.au

Animal Aid

my musing

Animal Aid is one of the world's longest established animal rights groups, having been founded in 1977. They campaign peacefully against all forms of animal abuse and promote cruelty-free living. Their vision is a world in which animals are no longer harmed and exploited for human gain, but allowed to live out their lives in peace.

website: Animalaid.org.uk

Whale and Dolphin Conservation

my musing

WDC has 30 years of experience conducting and supporting vital conservation, education and research projects around the globe. Their goal is always to work with local communities, prioritise non-invasive techniques and ensure that all research directly benefits the conservation of whales and dolphins.

website: Us.whales.org

Animal Equality

my musing

Animal Equality is an international animal advocacy organisation that is dedicated to defending animals through public education, campaigns and investigations.

website: Animalequality.org.uk

THE WILDLIFE TRUSTS

my musing

The Wildlife Trusts is a grassroots movement of people from a wide range of backgrounds and all walks of life, who believe that we need nature and nature needs us. They have more than 850,000 members, 38,000 volunteers, 2000 staff and 600 trustees.

website: Wildlifetrusts.org

WILDLIFE CONSERVATION SOCIETY (WCS)

my musing

WCS saves wildlife and wild places worldwide through science, conservation action, education and inspiring people to value nature. The WCS aims to ban the sale of ivory in the US.

website: Wcs.org

Interpeace

my musing

Interpeace is an international organisation that prevents violence and builds lasting peace, with 25 years of experience working in Africa, the Middle East, Asia, Europe and Latin America.

website: Interpeace.org

Human Rights Watch

my musing

Human Rights Watch provides timely information about human rights crises in more than 90 countries.

website: Hrw.org

my musing

As a global movement of over seven million people, Amnesty International is the world's largest grassroots human rights organisation. They investigate and expose abuses, educate and mobilise the public and help transform societies to create a safer, more just world. They received the Nobel Peace Prize for their life-saving work.

website: Amnesty.org.au

my musing

CARE is a global leader within a worldwide movement dedicated to ending poverty. They are known everywhere for their unshakeable commitment to the dignity of people. CARE works around the globe to save lives, defeat poverty and achieve social justice.

website: Care.org

Charity Water

my musing

Charity Water is a NYC-based charity working across 28 developing countries, bringing clean water to people in need.

website: Charitywater.org

Oxfam

my musing

Oxfam is a global movement of millions of people who share the belief that, in a world rich in resources, poverty isn't inevitable.

website: Oxfam.org.au

Plan International

my musing

Plan International works in more than 75 countries towards a just world that advances children's rights and equality for girls.

website: `Plan.org.au`

UN Women

my musing

UN Women is the UN body for gender equality and women's empowerment.

website: Unwomen.org.au

WALK IN HER SHOES

my musing

Walk in Her Shoes is a fundraising and team-building challenge to raise funds for CARE Australia. By signing up to Walk in Her Shoes and getting sponsored, you can raise funds to help create a more equal world for women and girls.

website: Walkinhershoes.org.au

my musing

Save the Children works in Australia, and around the world, to give a powerful voice to children and champion their rights. As a global organisation, in 2018 Save the Children directly reached more than 40 million children in 116 countries.

website: Savethechildren.org.au

Action Aid

my musing

Action Aid works across 45 countries and represents a global movement of women standing together to claim their human rights and campaign against injustice.

website: Actionaid.org.au

MALALA FUND

my musing

The Malala Fund is the official organisation led by Malala Yousafzai, focused on helping girls go to school and raise their voices for the right to education.

website: Malala.org

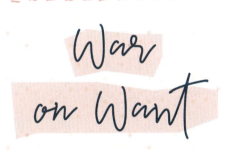

my musing

War on Want fights the root causes of poverty and human rights violations, as part of the worldwide movement for global justice.

website: Waronwant.org

The International Campaign to Ban Landmines

my musing

The International Campaign to Ban Landmines is a global network in some 100 countries that works for a world free of antipersonnel landmines, where landmine survivors can lead fulfilling lives.

website: icbl.org

WWF

my musing

For nearly 60 years, WWF has been protecting the future of nature. The world's leading conservation organisation, WWF works in 100 countries and is supported by close to five million members globally. WWF's unique way of working combines global reach with a foundation in science, involves action at every level from local to global, and ensures the delivery of innovative solutions that meet the needs of both people and nature.

website: Wwf.au

About
Lisa Messenger

Lisa Messenger is the vibrant, game-changing founder and CEO of *Collective Hub*.

She launched *Collective Hub* as a print magazine in 2013 with no experience, in an industry that people said was either dead or dying. Over the next seven years, *Collective Hub* grew into an international multimedia business and lifestyle platform with multiple verticals across print, digital, events and a co-working space – all of which served to ignite human potential.

For more than 19 years in her own businesses, Lisa has inspired game-changers, thought-leaders, style-makers, entrepreneurs and intrapreneurs across the world.

An international speaker and best-selling author, she is an authority on disruption in both the corporate sector and the start-up scene.

Lisa's experience in publishing has seen her produce more than 400 custom-published books for companies and individuals, as well as having authored and co-authored 27 herself.

Most notably, Lisa charted her ride to success post-launch of *Collective Hub,* documenting the journey and all its lessons in real time with her best-selling book *Daring & Disruptive: Unleashing the Entrepreneur*, and its sequels, which include *Life & Love: Creating the Dream; Money & Mindfulness: Living in Abundance; Break-ups & Breakthroughs: Turning an Ending Into a New Beginning; Purpose: Find Your Why and the How Will Look After Itself; Risk & Resilience, Breaking and Remaking a Brand; Work From Wherever: How to Set*

*Yourself Free and Still Achieve; and Daily Mantras
To Ignite Your Potential.*

Her passion is to challenge individuals and corporations to get out of their comfort zones, find their purpose, change the way they think, and to prove there is more than one way to do anything. She encourages creativity, innovation, and an entrepreneurial spirit, and lives life to the absolute max.

Most mornings she wakes up and pinches herself at how incredible her life is, but is also acutely aware and honest about life's bumps and tumbles along the way.

With fans including Sir Richard Branson and *New York Times* best-selling author Bradley Trevor Greive, and a social media following of more than 800,000 across her *Collective Hub* and personal platforms, Lisa's vision is to build a community of like-minded people who want to change the world.

In between being a serial entrepreneur, investor and avid traveller, she loves nothing more than being at home with her dog, Benny, doing some gardening, and collecting as many indoor plants as humanly possible.

EXTRAS

Collect all of Lisa Messenger's
books! Buy your copy at
www.collectivehub.com

Love this format?
See Lisa's other bite-sized best sellers,
Life in Lessons and *The Now of Work*
on **www.collectivehub.com**

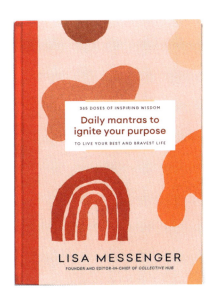

Learn from yesterday. Cherish today.
Dream big for tomorrow.
Buy your copy today at
www.collectivehub.com

Collective Hub's *Daily Gratitudes Planner* includes everything you need to create solid routines and be more grateful in every aspect of your life.

Available from
www.collectivehub.com

COLLECTIVE HUB
MAGAZINE

Collective Hub launched in 2013 as a print magazine in 37 countries, and quickly became a global sensation.

The brand evolved into a true international multimedia business and lifestyle platform that encompassed engaging digital content, bespoke events, strategic collaborations and unique product extensions.

Across it all, *Collective Hub*'s vision and purpose was to ignite human potential, and this mission will continue in any form the brand takes. Everything we produce exists to inspire and educate people on how to become the best versions of themselves, so that no human potential goes wasted.

EXTRAS

Combining style and substance with a fresh perspective on the issues that matter most, *Collective Hub* covers business, design, technology, social change, fashion, travel, food, film and art.

More than anything, *Collective Hub* was created to bring game-changers, thought-leaders, style-makers, entrepreneurs and intrapreneurs together. We offer pragmatism and inspiration in equal measure to help create a world of dreamers and doers. Join our community and unlock the best version of yourself.

To secure any back issues of *Collective Hub* magazine head to collectivehub.com

@collectivehub #collectivehub

EXTRAS

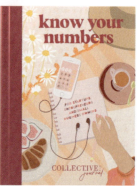

Love to journal? Check out Collective Hub's
*Create Your Best Life, The Ultimate Guide to Social
Media Marketing & Know your Numbers* journals.

Available from
www.collectivehub.com

Love to write or travel?
We love *Collective Hub* journals/planners!
The Ultimate Writer's Journal,
and *The Ultimate Travel Journal.*

Available from
www.collectivehub.com